KAREN BROWN'S

German Country Inns
& Castles

BOOKS IN KAREN BROWN'S COUNTRY INN SERIES

Austrian Country Inns & Castles

California Country Inns & Itineraries

English, Welsh & Scottish Country Inns

European Country Cuisine - Romantic Inns & Recipes

European Country Inns - Best on a Budget

French Country Bed & Breakfasts

French Country Inns & Chateaux

German Country Inns & Castles

Irish Country Inns

Italian Country Inns & Villas

Portuguese Country Inns & Pousadas

Scandinavian Country Inns & Manors

Spanish Country Inns & Paradors

Swiss Country Inns & Chalets

KAREN BROWN'S

German Country Inns
& Castles

Written by

KAREN BROWN and JUNE BROWN

Illustrated by

Barbara Tapp

Karen Brown's Country Inn Series

WARNER BOOKS

*TRAVEL PRESS editors: Clare Brown, June Brown,
Karen Brown, Iris Sandilands*

Cover painting and illustrations: Barbara Tapp

*This book is written in cooperation with:
Town and Country - Hillsdale Travel
16 East Third Avenue, San Mateo, California 94401*

*This Warner Books edition is published by arrangement with
Travel Press, San Mateo, California 94401*

Warner Books, Inc., 666 Fifth Avenue, New York, NY 10103
Ⓦ *A Warner Communications Company*

*Printed in the United States of America
First Warner Books Trade Paperback Printing: April 1988
10 9 8 7 6 5 4 3 2 1*

LIBRARY OF CONGRESS
Library of Congress Cataloging-in-Publication Data

Brown, Karen.
  German Country Inns & Castles / Karen Brown.
      p.   cm.
  Includes indexes
    ISBN 0-446-38815-7 (pbk.) (U.S.A.) / 0-446-38959-5(pbk.) (Canada)
    1. Hotels, taverns, etc. ·· Germany(West) ·· Guide-books.
    2. Castles ·· Germany (west) ·· Guide-books. 3. Germany (West)
-Description and travel   Guide-books. I. Title
  TX910.G4B76 1988
  647 .944301 ·· dc19   87-27234
                                          CIP

OAK HAVEN B&B

For Clare

Contents

HOTEL SECTION

INDEX OF HOTELS

Introduction

"ROMANTIK" is Germany's major promotional theme. The term translates as "romantic" - denoting the genius and passion of Germany's architects, artists, musicians and writers, and implying the richness and beauty of her landscape. But Germany is far more than just a beautiful romantic country of music and mountains. Germany is a prosperous country, her prosperity resulting from hard work, efficiency and prudence - characteristics displayed both in business and home life. This combination of a well-organized, tidy, clean, efficient country that also offers such romantic beauty creates a happy destination brimming with wonderful tourist possibilities to suit all tastes - whether it be cruising down the Rhine on a luxurious ship or hiking in Bavaria with a sandwich and bottle of wine tucked in a knapsack on your back. But no matter where you travel there are certain experiences you will bring home in your packet of memories which are typically "German" - regardless of the region explored: down comforters fluffed high on the beds of every inn; linens hanging from shuttered windows airing in the freshness of the cool morning air; breakfast buffets heaped with a tempting assortment of breads, salami, cheeses and jams; pretty barmaids carrying heavy steins of icy beer to laughing customers sitting at tables under the chestnut trees; hearty meals of good "home cooking" always served in all-too-generous portions; chambermaids scrubbing floors until they glisten; wood stacked so neatly, so perfectly, that one wonders if any logs less than perfect were discarded. You will also bring home the memory of the graciousness of the Germany people. "Gruss Gott" is a greeting that replaces "Guten Tag" or "Morgen" in regions bordering Austria, but regardless of the phrase or region, Germans are wonderful hosts and extend a warm welcome.

BEER

Germany's national drink, beer, is served at beer halls and taverns, particularly in the south of the country. Munich is the capital of beer drinking and a visit would not be complete without taking in the Hofbrauhaus beer hall and in summer visiting a German beer garden such as the one in the Englischer Garten. Brewed across the nation, the beers vary from light (helles) to dark (dunkles). From bottled beer served in glasses to foaming steins filled straight from the barrel, beer is drunk in copious quantities at all times.

BOATS

Koln-Dusseldorfer German Rhine Line (known as KD for short) operates cruises and ferry service on the Rhine and Moselle rivers. These excursions vary in duration from several hours to a week. No reservation is needed for ferry boat services - you buy your ticket from the pier before departure. The most popular day trips are: along the Rhine's most handsome stretch between Cologne and Mainz, the half day trip through the Rhine gorge between Koblenz and Mainz and along the Moselle river between Koblenz and Cochum. Schedules can be easily obtained while in Europe. For information on overnight cruises you can obtain a brochure from KD Cruise Line, 170 Hamilton Avenue, White Plains, NY 10601 or 323 Geary St., San Francisco, CA 94102.

BUSES

In conjunction with the German Railroad, buses make the trip along the "Romantic Road" between Fussen and Wurzburg. Principal stops include Rothenburg and Dinkelsbuhl. Additional service connects Mannheim, Heidelberg and Rothenburg. If you have a German Rail Card or a Eurailpass, the price of the bus ticket is included and you do not need to pay any supplement. The buses operate on a seasonal basis and their times are published in the Thomas Cook Continental Timetable - a reference guide used by most travel agents.

CREDIT CARDS

Many hotels do not accept plastic payment. Whether accommodation accepts payment by credit card is indicated in the accommodation description section using the terms: none, AX - American Express, DC - Diners Club, MC - Master Card and Access, VS - Visa, or simply, all major.

CURRENCY

The unit of currency in Germany is the Deutsche Mark, abbreviated to DM. 1 DM is equivalent to 100 Pfennigs. Banking hours vary but are usually open weekdays from 9:00 AM to 12:00 PM and again from 2:00 PM to 3:00 PM. Currency exchange offices are located at airports and railway stations in large cities. As a convenience to their guests and clients, hotels and department stores will also often convert foreign currency to Deutsche Marks.

DRIVING

BELTS: It is mandatory and strictly enforced in Germany that every passenger wear seatbelts. Children under twelve must not sit in the front seat.

CAR RENTALS: All major car rental companies are represented throughout Germany at airports and in the city areas. There is a definite price advantage to reserving and prepaying a car rental. Remember you will have to pay taxes and insurance locally. Also, depending on the policies and locations of a particular company, there are often surcharges for returning a car to a place other than the originating rental location. Automatic cars are usually available only in larger, more expensive models.

DRIVER'S LICENSE: Your local driver's license, which of course must be current, is accepted in Germany. Many people prefer to travel with an International Driver's License which is always an excellent idea although not mandatory. The minimum driving age is 18.

DRUNK DRIVING: It is a very serious offense to drive when you have been drinking. Anyone with an alcohol blood level of 0.8 % (less than two beers) is considered "under the influence".

GASOLINE: Gasoline is very expensive so budget this as part of your trip if you are driving.

ROADS: The German highway network consists of autobahns (similar to our freeways and marked with blue signs) and secondary roads (also excellent highways). Traffic moves fast on the autobahns where, unless signposted, there is no speed limit. On the secondary highways the speed limit is 62 miles or 100 kilometers per hour. The speed limit within city and town limits is usually 31 miles or 50 kilometers per hour.

ELECTRICITY

The voltage is 240. Most hotels have American-style razor points for 110 volts. If you want to take your favorite hairdryer, make certain it has dual voltage and purchase a kit of various sized and shaped electrical plugs.

ENGLISH

Many Germans speak some English. In large cities, airports, larger hotels and tourist destinations you will have no problem communicating in English, but in small towns, cafes, rural railway stations and the like, you may find that no English is spoken.

FESTIVALS AND FOLKLORE

With claim to such legends as "Snow White" and "The Pied Piper of Hamelin" and with a colorful history, the Germans can find numerous occasions for festivals and celebrations honoring everything from children saving a town from destruction to the completion of the grape harvest. Since these are staged over the course of the year, it would be difficult to experience them all on a limited holiday but it might prove rewarding to plan your travel dates to coincide with a particular festival. Some of the possibilities are the following:

BAD DURKHEIM - 2nd and 3rd Sundays in September - Germany's largest wine and sausage festival

BAD HARZBURG - April 30 - "Walpurgisfeier", the night the witches come to life for one night of merry celebration

BAD TOLZ - November 6 - "Leonhardiritt", a procession to honor the patron saint of animals

DINKELSBUHL - 3rd Monday in July - "Kinderzeche", a re-enactment of the children saving the town during the Thirty Years' War

HAMELIN - Sundays in July and August - a re-enactment of the Pied Piper spiriting away the town's children

HEIDELBERG - 1st Saturday in June, July and September - the castle is illuminated and fireworks are fired over the river

KOBLENZ-BRAUBACH - 2nd Saturday in August - "The Rhine in Flames": the Rhine valley between the towns of Koblenz and Braubach is lit by bonfires and floodlights

MUNICH - end of September and early October - "Oktoberfest", the world's biggest beer festival

ROTHENBURG - one Sunday a month in summer - "Maistertruk", a re-enactment of the drinking feat that saved the town from destruction during the Thirty Years' War

ULM - Mondays in July - "Fischerstechen", jousting on boats

FOOD

Food in Germany is plentiful and an irresistible temptation. Consider eating both a dining and social event. Rationalize that to visit Germany and not frequent a beerhall or relax at a sidewalk cafe and savor a "kuchen mit schlag" (pastry with whipped cream) would be to deny yourself a truly German experience. South of Frankfurt the menus highlight a variety of sausages, pork, salads, potatoes, dumplings or noodles; while in the north, fresh seafoods, vegetables, meat and ham dominate the selections. There are eating places available for any budget, from inexpensive sausage stands to plush elegant restaurants.

Breakfast or "Fruhstuck" is a plentiful assortment of delicious rolls, wurst or sausages, pates, cheeses, homemade jams, country butter and often cereals, yoghurt or fresh cream. Lunch or "Mittagessen" is the main meal in Germany. Served customarily from noon to 2:00 PM, it generally consists of soup, meat and vegetables. However, when traveling, you might opt to save valuable afternoon time by stopping at a pub or beer hall for a simpler fare of hot sausage, sauerkraut and homefried potatoes accompanied by a glass of cold beer, or enjoying a hot wurst sold by street vendors. Afternoon coffee or "Kaffee" is popular, especially on weekends, and is served approximately from 4:00 to 5:00 PM. Pastries and cakes are served "mit schlag", a thick helping of cream that makes any regional specialty a sinful delight. Dinner or "Abendessen" is usually enjoyed between 6:00 and 9:00 PM. When served at home it is usually a lighter meal but in restaurants you will find the same type of meals as at midday.

The food is plentiful. Most countryside inns cultivate small gardens which provide the delicious salads and vegetables. Jams are often homemade, breads usually fresh from the oven. The hotel owners are frequently the chefs, and, if not, closely supervise the preparation of food. Forget your diet: the fare is hearty and bountiful. All your walking will easily compensate for a little indulgence. Except in tourist centers, the menus are printed only in German so take your dictionary to dinner with you.

GEOGRAPHY

This guide covers West Germany and the walled city of West Berlin deep within East German territory. Germany is a large European country when compared to her neighbors the Netherlands, Belgium, Luxembourg, Switzerland, Austria and Czechoslovakia, yet small in size when compared to America. Within her 530 miles length and 144 miles breadth there is great geographic diversity, from the sand dunes of northern islands across heathered heathlands, through the thick forests where the Brothers Grimm found Sleeping Beauty, beneath castles along the Rhine gorge, along the picturesque Romantic Road and over the Bavarian plateau to the towering Alps.

HISTORY

Germany has always been a country of shifting frontiers. Since Roman times the country was continually subdivided in an ever-changing mosaic of "units" of different degrees of political importance. These "units" comprised states, kingdoms, Hanseatic cities, free towns, principalities and ecclesiastical fiefs. Held together by leagues, reichs, confederations and empires, German history fills vast volumes of European history. In 1871 Germany became a united country and this unity lasted until 1945 when the country was occupied by Britain, France, America and Russia (the Allies) at the conclusion of World War II. In 1949 the British, French and American sectors were linked as the German Federal Republic - West Germany. The Russian sector developed into the German Democratic Republic - East Germany.

This divided nation has been home to some of the world's most influential leaders: Charlemagne, Frederick Barbarossa, Otto the Great, Martin Luther, Frederick the Great, Bismarck and Adolph Hitler. Although there has been an impressive list of German leaders who have shaped world history, it is Ludwig II, King of Bavaria, who is most often remembered by tourists. Ruling Bavaria between 1864 and 1886, Ludwig II is fondly known as Mad King Ludwig. A notable patron of art and music, he idolized and subsidized the composer Richard Wagner. Lonely, eccentric, cut off from the mainstream of world politics and obsessed by the glories of the past, Ludwig sought solace in a fanciful building scheme - his Bavarian castles of Neuschwanstein, Herrenchiemsee and Linderhof. His building extravaganzas brought Bavaria to the brink of bankruptcy and, before he could begin on further palaces, he was declared unfit to rule by reason of insanity. Within a week of his deposition Ludwig drowned in Lake Starnberg (under circumstances always shaded with mystery). Your own travels will be enriched if you do some reading before your departure to both comprehend and associate all that you will see and experience.

HOLIDAY ROUTES

Germany has a network of holiday routes that allow visitors to follow special interest, scenic and historical routes. All are signposted and indicated on most maps. A sampling of the more popular routes are:

BURGENSTRASSE - the Castle Highway between Mannheim and Nuremberg

DEUTSCHE ALPENSTRASSE - the German Alpine Way between Berchtesgaden and Lindau

DEUTSCHE MARCHENSTRASSE - the German Fairytale Route between Hanau and Bremen

DEUTSCHE WEINSTRASSE - the German Wine Road between Schweigen and Bockenheim

MOSELWEINSTRASSE - the Moselle River Wine Route between Trier and Koblenz

ROMANTISCHE STRASSE - the Romantic Road between Wurzburg and Fussen

SCHWARZWALD HOCHSTRASSE - the Black Forest High Road between Baden-Baden and Freudenstadt

HOTEL DESCRIPTIONS

This book is divided into two sections with hotel descriptions in both. The first portion of the book outlines itineraries and a hotel with a brief description is suggested for each destination. The second section of the book is a complete list of places to stay, appearing alphabetically by town. The list provides a wide selection of hotels throughout Germany. A brief description, an illustration and pertinent information is provided on each one.

RATES are those quoted to us for the 1988 summer season. The rates given are for the LEAST expensive single room and the MOST expensive double room inclusive of breakfast, all service charges and taxes. Some hotels have two-room suites at higher prices. Please ALWAYS CHECK prices and terms when making a reservation. Rates are quoted in Deutsche Marks.

RESERVATIONS should always be made in advance for the major tourist cities during the peak season of June through September. Hotel space in the cities is especially crowded, particularly during certain events such as the Munich Oktoberfest or the Passion Play performed every ten years in Oberammergau. So unless you don't mind taking your chances on a last-minute cancellation or staying on the outskirts of a town, make a reservation. Space in the countryside is a little easier. If you have your heart set on some special little inn, to avoid disappointment, make a reservation either by phone or in writing. Reservations are confining. Most hotels will want a deposit to hold your room and frequently refunds are difficult should you change your plans - especially at the last minute. Whenever a hotel has a United States reservations office we have included the name and phone number - note that sometimes they book only the most expensive rooms or quote a higher price to protect themselves against currency fluctuations.

ITINERARIES

The first section of this guide outlines itineraries throughout Germany. You should be able to find an itinerary, or section of an itinerary, to fit your exact time frame and suit your own particular interests. You can custom tailor your own vacation by combining segments of itineraries or using two "back to back".

The itineraries do not indicate a specific number of nights at each destination. We cannot, however, help adding our recommendation: do not rush. Learn to travel as the Europeans do. Allow sufficient time to settle into a hotel properly and absorb the special ambiance each has to offer. If the hotels we suggest seem over your budget, or just not for you, you can enjoy the holiday by following our sightseeing suggestions and substituting your own accommodation.

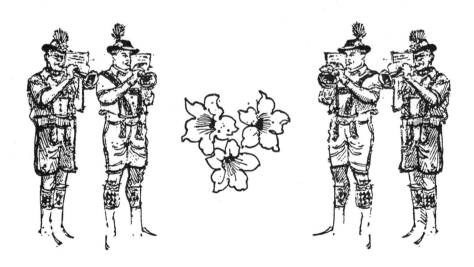

MAPS

At the beginning of each itinerary a map shows the itinerary's routing. This should be considered as no more than an overview. To supplement our routings you will need a set of detailed maps which will indicate all of the highway numbers, autobahns, alternative little roads, autobahn access points and exact mileages. Our suggestion would be to purchase a comprehensive selection of both city maps and regional maps before your departure, and with a highlight pen mark your own "personalized" itinerary and pinpoint your city hotels. The Michelin maps are exceptionally good.

SHOPPING

Most shops are open Monday through Friday from 9:00 AM to 6:00 PM and Saturday till noon or 2:00 PM. Many small shops close for an hour or two in the middle of the day when the shopkeeper goes home for lunch. In resort areas, some of the shops are open seven days a week.

You will discover the same consistently high standard of products throughout Germany as a group of well known manufacturers distribute their products nationwide. Price variations are minimal. The department stores are large and display a magnificent assortment of items. In the cities some of Germany's larger department store chains to watch for are Kaufhof, Hertie, Karstadt and Horten, as they usually have an excellent souvenir department and competitive prices.

Some favorite items to take home are:

CAMERAS: German cameras are magnificent, with Leica perhaps the most famous name.

CARS: With Germany the home of Volkswagen, Porsche, Mercedes and BMW, many travelers consider purchasing a car while in Europe. Generally the more expensive the car the greater the savings. A great deal of advanced planning is required to select, insure and ship your car. Back home your car is a daily reminder of your German vacation.

CHINA: Nymphenberg and Rosenthal china is exquisite and expensive.

CLOCKS: From the region of the Black Forest come the charming traditional cuckoo clocks and the handsome desk clocks.

CLOTHES: Good quality high-fashion items can be bought at very reasonable costs. Sizes vary slightly so you should always try clothes on. The main fashion centers are Munich and Dusseldorf.

DIRNDLS: From the region of Bavaria, dirndls are charming pinafores usually of provincial print material worn with a white blouse and apron. All sizes are available from adorable tiny dresses for little girls to matching costumes for mommy and grandmother. In addition to all sizes, the dresses come in all fabrics and designs from gay daytime cotton models to fabulous pure silk high-fashion designer creations.

KNITWEAR: Hand-knitted sweaters, jackets and heavy wool knee socks are typical of the southern Alpine regions of Germany.

LEATHER GOODS: German leather goods are especially beautiful. The skirts, jackets and luggage are expensive, but absolutely gorgeous. A trip to southern Germany would not be complete without bringing home a pair of "Lederhosen", the wonderful leather shorts for all the men and little boys in the family.

POTTERY: Beer steins make a wonderful souvenir from a German vacation. From Goebel come the whimsical Hummel figurines of Bavarian children in lederhosen and dirndls.

TOYS: Marvelous wooden toys for babies and small children are easy to tuck into the unoccupied spaces of your suitcase and fun to bring home as gifts. Especially appealing to children of all ages are the Stieff animals with the yellow button in their ear, available throughout Germany. It is possible to visit the factory in Giengen where these famous stuffed animals are made and find some bargains in their seconds shop.

WOOD: From Bavaria come tinkling music boxes and religious carvings. Nativity scenes and wooden Christmas tree ornaments make wonderful gifts.

If you are planning to do much shopping, you should also plan to take advantage of the tax credit. Germany has a 14% Value Added Tax which is refundable if you buy over 200 DM of goods, so ask for a tax refund form. Department and larger stores will carry them but in the hinterlands they will not know what you are talking about, so in those cases keep your receipts and goods and then obtain forms from the customs office. As you leave the country you MUST have this form stamped by the German customs official at the airport or border crossings. If you are leaving by train, you must get off the train at the border and have the customs inspector stamp the form. Keep your purchases together because the customs agent will probably want to see what you have bought. You mail the form back to the store from which you made the purchases and they will reimburse the tax you paid in Deutsche Marks to your home address. If you buy goods and the store ships them out of the country you will not be charged the Value Added Tax.

TELEPHONES

Calls from hotels are often expensive due to a surcharge system. It is best to confirm with the hotel whether or not there is an additional charge. The easiest way to make an international phone call is to go to a major post office where the attendant makes arrangements for your call and you pay when it is completed. Rates from North America to Europe are about half the cost of Europe to North America.

TOURIST INFORMATION

The big, blue I denotes the location of the tourist information booths in all major towns, train stations, airports and tourist centers across Germany. Information can be obtained before you go from the German National Tourist Offices, 747 Third Avenue, 33rd Floor, New York, NY 10017; or 444 S. Flower Street, Suite 2230, Los Angeles, CA 90071.

TRAINS

From the high-speed "Rheingold Express" to the local trains that stop in every little village, Germany has a rail system that is easy to use, operates on time and embraces over 18,000 miles of track, enabling the tourist to criss-cross the nation with ease. Trains arrive and depart with clockwork-like precision. The cars are marked on the outside with their destination, first and second class, and within each there are seating areas for smoking and no smoking. Most trains of substantial size have a dining car, while those that do not often have a man who walks through selling snacks and drinks.

In each train station there is usually an information desk where someone speaks English to assist you with schedules. Other services at large stations include currency exchange, accommodation information, shops and restaurants. Baggage carts are free and in plentiful supply at larger stations. For trains within Germany you can buy individual tickets, use your Eurailpass or buy a German Rail Card. The German Rail Card permits unlimited rail travel for four, nine or sixteen days. It also allows free travel on buses along the "Romantic Road" and reductions on river steamers on the Rhine and Moselle rivers. The Eurailpass is a bargain for those who are traveling extensively in Europe. For further information contact the German Federal Railroad, 747 Third Avenue, New York, NY 10017.

UMLAUTS

Umlauts are a grammatical punctuation that appear as two dots above a vowel identifying a particular sound. An "e" immediately following the identified vowel will achieve the same result. Our printing facilities do not include the use of an umlaut, and yet we were concerned as to whether or not to add the "e" to achieve the proper Germanic spelling of a word. As most people would not realize the significance of the umlaut and read the addition of the "e" as a spelling change, we decided it best to ignore the umlaut altogether in the hopes of simplifying the text, avoiding any confusion and trusting that those with a working knowledge of the German language will forgive and understand our grammatical omission.

WEATHER

Rainfall occurs at all times of year. Autumn is mild and long, spring chilly and late, winter often snowy and cold and summer can vary from cloudless and balmy through hot and muggy to cold and wet. Be prepared for chilly weather with woolly sweaters and a raincoat that can be taken off as the day warms and clears and enjoy Germany rain or shine, snow or sun, cold or warm.

WINES

The eleven German wine-growing regions stretch from Bonn south to Lake Constance. Most of the wine is white wine. Each region produces a wine that is similar in taste to other wines of that region yet differs from wines produced in other parts of Germany. The wine regions often have a signposted route that combines sights and wineries in such a way that you work up a proper thirst. You can sample wines by the glass in taverns - weinstube and weinhaus. Restaurants offer house wines served in pottery jugs, and bottles can be selected from the wine list. But the most appealing way to celebrate German wines is to attend one of the more than 500 wine festivals that take place in the wine regions from July to late October - the German Tourist Office can give you details about festivals and tours.

When looking at German wine lists, selecting an appropriate bottle often seems a daunting task. If you can see the wine labels your job is made much easier. The label tells you the district, producer, type of grape used and the year it was bottled. In addition, look for labels with yellow borders, or backgrounds, to denote dry wine and those with lime green to denote semi-dry wine. Sometimes the labels are not color-coded and the word "trocken" indicates dry and "halbtrocken" semi-dry. Labels grade the wine into "tafelwein" - tablewine, "qualitatswein" - quality wine and "qualitatswein mit pradikt" - quality wine with special attributes. Some of the wine regions also have special glasses "just for their wine" such as the green colored wine glass of the Rhine and the amber colored wine glass of the Moselle.

Germany by Rail, Boat and Bus

COLOGNE

Rhine River

Koblenz • Lorely
Oberwesel ★ **ASSMANNSHAUSEN**
Rudesheim ★ ★ ★ Frankfurt
Oestrich

HEIDELBERG

ROTHENBURG
★ Feuchtwangen
● Dinkelsbuhl
Schwabisch ★ Nordlingen
Hall ● Harburg
● Donauworth

Augsburg

Weilheim **MUNICH**
Oberammergau
Pfronten ★ Fussen ★ Murnau
Neuschwanstein **GARMISCH-PARTENKIRCHEN**
Linderhof Mittenwald
Zugspitze

France
Switzerland

East Germany

Hamburg
Cologne
Frankfurt
Munich

● Overnight Stops
★ Alternate Hotel Choices
See Hotel Section of Guide
⛴ Boat 🚌 Bus ✈ Airport

19

Germany by Rail, Boat and Bus

Sit back, relax and enjoy traveling through Germany by rail, boat and bus. This itinerary was designed to link some of Germany's loveliest destinations in such a way that the transportation becomes part of the sightseeing experience. How much more enjoyable to savor the Rhine from the deck of a boat, or sit on a train or bus enjoying the scenery knowing that no one has to concentrate on the road. Frequently the lasting impressions you have of a holiday are of the people you have met and there is no better opportunity to get to know Germans and visitors from around the world than by traveling with them. The German Rail Card is the most convenient ticket for this itinerary. If you are also traveling elsewhere in Europe, consider the Eurailpass. Either card will relieve you of the frustration of purchasing point-to-point train tickets plus entitle you to free bus transportation on the Romantic Road or Castle Road buses and reductions in the cost of river steamers. The key to carefree travel is to pack lightly and limit yourself to one small suitcase. While all German stations provide luggage carts, more often than not there are long flights of steps to negotiate.

The Pfalz
Rhine River

In the following itinerary approximate train and boat times have been included. Please note that these are given as a reference to show how the itinerary fits together. Schedules are constantly changing, so these must be verified. Also boat, bus and some train services are seasonal, so be very meticulous in making your plans. All the times of trains, boats and buses used in this itinerary can be checked in a Thomas Cook Continental Timetable.

Below are a few helpful words to know when traveling by public transportation.

BAHNHOF: Train station
SCHIFFAHRT: Boat dock
ABFAHRT: Time of departure
NACH: Travelling to
BAHNSTEIG: Platform number at the train station
GLEIS: Track number

With these few terms you should be in business.

ORIGINATING CITY   COLOGNE

Cologne is a delightful starting point for any vacation. A beguiling blending of old with new, a town just perfect for walking and a populace that welcomes visitors combine to make this city a favorite. This prosperous town and port were a prime target of Allied bombers during the Second World War. Looking at the reconstructed city today, it is hard to realise that over 90 percent of the city was flattened.

The Dom (Cologne Cathedral) occupies a square that is the heart of the city. Beloved by all, the cathedral's twin steeples and delicate twin spires are the city's landmark. The building is as beautiful inside as out. Next door to the cathedral, the Roman Museum is a must: its fabulous mosaic floor dates from the 2nd century and its mock-ups of rooms in Roman houses are an easy, interesting way to get a feel for life in Roman times. The main shopping street, the Hohenstrasse, runs south from the cathedral and connects into the other main shopping street, the Schildergasse, which turns west towards the Neumarkt Square. All the major museums and churches are within easy walking distance of these two streets. Spend your day sightseeing and leave the evening free to explore the quaint old town that fronts the River Rhine. Here, set on narrow streets, you will find slender, gaily painted houses filled with bars and restaurants.

If you are taking the early morning ferry, you will probably want to overnight in Cologne. There are two hotel recommendations, each quite different in facilities and ambiance. The HAUS LYSKIRCHEN, located just a few minutes' walk from center of the town near the River Rhine, is very simple, yet quiet and sedate. The hotel blends stark modern with country decor in a way that is not jarring. If you prefer a deluxe hotel, stay instead at the DOM HOTEL. Although large and expensive, the Dom Hotel has a superb location in the center of town (if this is your choice, request a room with a view of the cathedral).

DESTINATION I   ASSMANNSHAUSSEN   Hotel Krone

The majority of the tourist boats that ply the River Rhine are operated by the Koln-Dusseldorfer Rhine Line with its familiar KD symbol. Their office is located by the river in front of the old town, between the Hohenzollern and the Koln-Deutzer bridges. Here you purchase your boat ticket for the Rhine river trip between

Cologne and Assmannshaussen. (You will receive a discount if you have a Eurailpass or a German Rail Card). It is not necessary to buy your ticket before you arrive in Cologne, but do so during your stay. When you obtain your ticket, verify the time of departure and find out from which dock your boat sails.

7:00 AM depart Cologne by KD boat
5:50 PM arrive Assmannshausen

You have an early start today, but once you are settled on board you can leisurely eat breakfast as you enjoy the scenery. Your modern boat is equipped for all weather: if it looks as though the day will be warm and clear, you can find a seat on the open deck; if it is cool and raining, you can watch the river churn by from the snug comfort of one of the heated lounges. Fabled for its beauty, the Rhine presents one vista after another. Majestic castles present themselves to be photographed, steep vineyard-covered banks slide by and picturesque towns and villages huddle along the river edge.

The loveliest section of the Rhine lies between KOBLENZ and ASSMANNS-HAUSEN for here the valley is at its narrowest, with steep banks enclosing the river in walls of green and once mighty castles looming on hilltops. As the boat slows to navigate the narrowest part of the gorge the fabled LORELEI cliff rises before you. Legend has it that the beautiful Lorelei, sitting atop her rock combing her golden tresses, so entranced the sailors with her singing that the rules of navigation were forgotten and their ships were dashed onto the rocks.

There are many other legends told about this section of the Rhine, such as the story of the STERRENBERG and LIEBENSTEIN castles perched side by side high above the river bank. These castles supposedly belonged to two brothers whose hatred of each other was so intense that they built a high wall between their two adjacent forts. Another tale is of the seven maidens of OBERWESEL castle. These pretty young damsels were so hard-hearted towards their suitors that the river capsized their boat and turned them into seven rocks.

Arriving at Assmannshausen, it is a five-minute walk to the HOTEL KRONE. Upon request, the hotel will send someone to the pier to meet you and help you with your luggage. The hotel's vine-covered terrace and raised restaurant provide lovely places for dining and watching life as it passes on the busy river. This lovely old hotel is sandwiched between the railway tracks and the river: you will get the best night's sleep by requesting a river-facing room in the hotel annex. The location of the Hotel Krone is superb, the dining room very attractive and the wisteria-covered terrace a romantic oasis, but do not expect much from the bedrooms - none are outstanding in decor. The rooms in the original inn have more character than those in the annex - although their bathrooms are across the hall.

Hotel Krone
Assmannshaussen

Germany by Rail, Boat and Bus

Allow some time this morning to explore the quaint old streets of Assmannshausen, then take a short taxi ride to the nearby town of RUDESHEIM to continue your journey by train.   Plan to arrive early at the station, leave your bags in a baggage locker and explore Rudesheim.   Visit the BROMSERBERG CASTLE, located only a few steps from the train station on the Rhine River Road.   The castle is now a splendid wine museum filled with artifacts pertaining to the production of wine from the earliest days.   A short stroll farther along the river brings you to the picturesque Drosselgasse.   Here, on what is reputed to be the jolliest street in the world, one wine tavern props up another.   Even if you do not partake of the wine, it is fun to wander along this festive street.

12:40 PM depart Rudesheim by train
2:12 PM arrive Heidelberg

Paralleling the river, the train passes through the vineyards of the Rheingau before turning south to HEIDELBERG.   The tourist information office is just outside the train station, so pick up information pamphlets before taking a taxi to the ZUM RITTER hotel.   The hotel's intricate Renaissance facade was built in 1592 and is a sightseeing attraction in itself.   The hotel is definitely the most beguiling in town; however, although its restaurant is bursting with olde worlde charm, the bedrooms are rather spartan.   But the location is perfect - at the very heart of this effervescent town.

History has been kind to Heidelberg: unlike so many less fortunate German cities, it has been spared the ravages of recent wars.   Surprisingly though, it was the romantic operetta "The Student Prince" that put Heidelberg on the tourist map. The streets of its old town are a maze of cozy restaurants and lively student taverns. Above the town looms the famous ruins of its picture-postcard-perfect castle: you can walk up to the castle, but it is easier and more fun to take the mountain railway from the Kornmarkt. The castle is now mostly a ruin, but still great fun to explore, and offers spectacular views of the town and the river from the terrace. The very best views of the castle and the town are from the Philosophers' Walk on the northern bank of the Neckar river. Cross the Alte Bridge spanning the Neckar and the Philosophers' Walk is clearly indicated by signs.

Boat lovers will enjoy a boat trip along the Neckar river. Operating only in summer, these go round trip from Heidelberg to NECKARGEMUND.

Hotel Zum Ritter
Heidelberg

Germany by Rail, Boat and Bus

There is excellent train service between Heidelberg and MUNICH but the fastest and most luxurious is provided by the "TEE RHEINGOLD", the Rheingold Express, that travels at speeds up to 125 miles per hour.

12:44 PM depart Heidelberg by the TEE RHEINGOLD
3:45 PM arrive Munich

As you travel aboard one of Europe's most luxurious inter-city trains, the countryside whisks by and you soon find yourself at Munich's Hauptbahnhof. Before you leave the train station, visit the tourist office where you will be gladly supplied with maps and information.   Your hotel is just a streetcar ride away and if you prefer this to a taxi ride, the tourist office will give you instructions on how to get there.

The SPLENDID HOTEL, truly worthy of its name, is a splendid little hotel evoking the ambiance of a country home.   The lobby is intimate - elegantly refined and charmingly decorated with comfortable, traditional furnishings.   Although there is no restaurant, breakfast is served either in your bedroom or in the lounge - or best yet, when the weather is balmy, breakfast is served in the charming garden courtyard.   The Splendid Hotel is not in the very heart of Munich, but just a comfortable walk away along an elegant shop-lined boulevard.

Munich has something to offer everyone, so be generous with your time in Germany's most popular city.   You must visit the Marienplatz.   Plan on being there at 11 AM for the glockenspiel performance.   As the clock on the town hall facade chimes eleven, little enameled copper figures emerge from arches around the clock and perform a jousting tournament.   The cameras click; the crowds disperse.   The show is wonderful but Munich has many other attractions: fine buildings of all periods, renowned shopping streets, numerous magnificent museums filled with priceless treasures, music, theater, beer gardens under massive chestnut trees where quarts of beer and enormous pretzels are merrily served and consumed, beer halls like the Hofbrauhaus (Munich's largest), and the Viktualienmarkt filled with sausage stands, fruits and flowers. But Munich's greatest attraction is the Oktoberfest, sixteen days of merriment that ends on the first Sunday in October. What began as a wedding celebration in 1810 when Prince Ludwig married, has grown to be the world's largest folk festival. For further sightseeing suggestions please see Bavarian Highlights page 83.

*Splendid Hotel
Munich*

DESTINATION IV   GARMISCH-PARTENKIRCHEN   Clausing's Posthotel

When you are ready to leave Munich there is frequent train service to GARMISCH-PARTENKIRCHEN, so the following is just a suggestion.

2:00 PM depart Munich by train
3:19 PM arrive Garmisch-Partenkirchen

Lakes and mountains come into view as the train approaches Garmisch-Partenkirchen, considered one town yet in actuality two: Partenkirchen on one side of the railway track and Garmisch on the other. Garmisch is beautiful. No matter what time of year you come, the high Alpine peaks ringing the town provide a spectacularly beautiful setting and opportunities for skiing in the winter or hiking in the summer.

CLAUSING'S POSTHOTEL has a central location within Garmisch. Its pink stucco facade has a deeply overhanging roof that protects a lineup of 18th- century statues set in between the upper floor windows. With a trio of antique-clad dining rooms and an array of lovely guest rooms, Clausing's Posthotel provides a wonderful base for explorations of this especially picturesque area of Germany.

Although the less energetic can admire the view from a cable car window, Garmisch-Partenkirchen is a walker's paradise. Germans love to walk and you can join them on the well-marked trails, one of the loveliest of which is through the PARTNACHKLAMM VALLEY. Follow the road to the right of the Olympic ski stadium and take the Graseckbahn cable car to the FORSTHAUS GRASECK. From here a trail leads to the narrow Partnachklamm gorge. You walk along a rocky ledge with a guardrail between you and the tumbling river, sometimes passing through rock tunnels and behind cascading waterfalls. You get a little wet and the gorge is chilly even in summer, but the experience is breathtaking. As you leave the gorge you pay a modest toll and find yourself back on the road leading to the Olympic ski stadium.

Not surprisingly, the finest view in Germany is from atop its highest mountain, the ZUGSPITZE - remember to take warm sweaters for this excursion. The Zugspitze cog railway departs from the Zugspitzebahnhof, next to the main railway, almost every hour on the hour. The train ascends through the valley and brings you out at the HOTEL SCHEEFERNERHAUS below the summit of the Zugspitze. The train trip takes about an hour so try and plan your arrival to coincide with lunch at this scenic spot - a cable car departs about every half hour and whisks you the last 2 miles up the mountain. Enjoy the view, soak up the high Alpine sunshine and return to the valley on the other cable car for the ten-minute descent to the EIBSEE lake. From Eibsee you take a bus or taxi back into town.

King Ludwig II of Bavaria intended to ring his kingdom with five fanciful castles. Only three were partially completed before his death at age 40 in 1886. Raised in isolation at HOHENSCHWANGAU, Ludwig began his reign with great promise at the young age of 18. Before long, though, his interest in politics diminished and, in a vain pursuit of happiness, he embarked on his monumental building spree. The expense of the program and Ludwig's erratic behavior alarmed the government, who feared (probably justifiably) that Ludwig might bankrupt the country with his wildly extravagant projects. So they declared Ludwig unfit to rule by reason of insanity. Four days later Ludwig was found drowned under mysterious circumstances - supposedly suicide, but the world still wonders, "who done it?". But today the tourist benefits, as all of Ludwig's palaces are now museums. Of the three, NEUSCHWANSTEIN is a MUST. On Mondays and Wednesdays a coach tour, leaving from Garmisch, incorporates a visit to Neuschwanstein and the adjacent Hohenschwangau Castle with a drive through the nearby towns of Fussen and Oberammergau.

Many Americans will immediately recognize Neuschwanstein, located high above the valley atop a rocky ledge, as being the inspiration for Walt Disney's Sleeping Beauty's Castle at Disneyland and Disneyworld. You begin to appreciate the effort that went into building this castle as you walk up the steep path to the fortress high above. The only way to decrease a half-hour uphill hike to a ten-minute one is to take a shuttle bus or horsedrawn wagon part-way to the castle.

In summer you may have to wait in long lines to tour the castle's fanciful interior, for this is understandably one of Germany's most popular sightseeing attractions. Designed by a theater set designer and an eccentric king, the interior is a romantic flight of fancy whose rooms afford spectacular views of Alpine lakes and snowy peaks. Ludwig greatly admired Richard Wagner and scenes from his operas are found throughout the decor.

At the end of the castle tour, if you are not too tired, walk up the Pollat Gorge to the Marienbrucke which spans the ravine above the castle: you will be rewarded with a spectacular view of the castle.

From the road at the foot of the castle, it is a short walk to King Ludwig's childhood home, Hohenschwangau Castle. Though the interior is somewhat heavy, it has a homey quality to it. It was here that Ludwig met his adored Wagner and it was here that the young king lived while he kept a watchful eye on the building progress at Neuschwanstein.

Note: If your visit to Garmisch does not coincide with the coach tour, you can still visit the castle using the local bus to FUSSEN which leaves from the bus station at 8.00 AM and drops you at the castle at 9.30 AM. The early arrival means that you avoid the crowds. Upon arrival, visit the castle and take an afternoon bus into Fussen. The return bus to Garmisch leaves Fussen in the early evening.

LINDERHOF, the smallest of the three castles, is an afternoon bus tour from Garmisch. The low-lying building contains an opulent French rococo interior. But it is the formal Italian baroque gardens with their pools and cascades, formal flower beds and clipped box hedges that are most pleasing. The tour also includes OBERAMMERGAU, a village of traditional-style painted houses, home of the world-famous Passion Play, performed by the villagers every decade in the years ending with zero. The Passion Play was first performed in 1634 and has been performed consistently ever since. The town is loyal to the vow they made to God that if he protected their town from the Plague, they in turn would stage a religious play in thanksgiving. Every ten years the town bustles with activity as everyone in the village is involved in one way or another with the production.   Oberammergau is also famous for its lovely wood carvings - a tradition which keeps the villagers busy between plays.

Ludwig's third castle, HERRENCHIEMSEE, was modeled on the French palace of Versailles.   Lying beyond this itinerary, it is found on an island in the middle of the CHIEMSEE.

Ringed by the Karwendel mountains, MITTENWALD is but a short train ride from Garmisch.   From the Mittenwald railway station it is a delightful walk around this small town, known not only as a holiday resort, but also as a violin makers' village. Mittenwald violins are famous throughout the world and the Geigenbau (violin) Museum is well worth a visit.

Garmisch-Partenkirchen
Clausing's Posthotel

There are several train connections from Garmisch-Partenkirchen to Rothenburg, but if you want to incorporate the fun of sightseeing along the "Romantic Road", you must make an early start.

7:34 AM depart Garmisch-Partenkirchen by train
8:12 AM arrive Weilheim

8:17 AM depart Weilheim by train
9:33 AM arrive Augsburg

10:20 AM depart Augsburg by bus
3:15 PM arrive Rothenburg

German trains arrive and depart with precision, so do not worry about missing your train connection in WEILHEIM.   You can speed your transfer between trains by asking the information office in Garmisch from which platform the AUGSBURG train departs.

In Augsburg the German Rail bus that runs the length of the Romantic Road leaves from in front of the railway station.   If you have a Eurailpass or German Rail Card the bus is free and you pay only a small fee for the transportation of your bag. Otherwise the bus ticket is purchased on the bus.

The 10:20 AM bus originates in Munich and operates daily from March 17th to November 5th.   In the unlikely event that the bus is filled, an additional bus departs at 11:10 AM.   This bus originates in Fussen and operates from June 3rd to September 30th.

The Romantic Road bus driver is accompanied by a charming hostess who gives a multi-lingual commentary on the places of interest you pass en route.

The further north the bus travels, the more picturesque the scenery and the towns. Passing through DONAUWORTH and HARBURG, the bus then stops briefly to pick up and drop off passengers in NORDLINGEN and WALLERSTEIN and arrives in DINKELSBUHL in time for lunch.

You will find Dinkelsbuhl a delightful small town of medieval gabled houses and cobbled streets encircled by a formidable wall. The long lunch stop gives you plenty of time for food, shopping and sightseeing. Many towns in this area were defeated and destroyed during the Thirty Years' War: Dinkelsbuhl was conquered but saved from destruction by the children who pleaded with the conquering Swedes to spare their town. Every July the town commemorates the bravery of its children with the "Kinderzeche" (children's festival). Amble about - down narrow cobblestoned streets, by picture-perfect little houses with their steep-peaked roofs and window boxes overflowing with flowers, and under painted oriel windows protruding from old houses' upper stories.

The bus continues down lovely country roads and through rolling countryside that becomes more beautiful as the day progresses. Saving the very best for last, you enter through the old city gates into ROTHENBURG. Walking down the cobblestoned streets of Rothenburg is rather like taking a stroll through an open-air museum: there is history in every stone. Old houses, towers and gateways that have withstood the ravages of the centuries are there for you to explore. Tourists throng the streets but somehow the town has the ability to absorb them and not let their numbers spoil its beauty.

The ROMANTIK HOTEL MARKUSTURM is a particularly lovely old house next to one of the old city gates, a superb location for exploring this very wonderful medieval town. Fitting right in with the cozy atmosphere of the town and with a selection of lovely traditional and modern bedrooms, the Hotel Markusturm makes a nice choice for a hotel in Rothenburg.

Rothenburg has narrowly escaped destruction on several occasions. During the Thirty Years' War, General Tilly laid siege to the town and, despite spirited resistance, breached the walls. Tilly demanded that the town be destroyed and its councillors put to death. He assembled the town councillors to pass sentence on the town and was offered a drink from the town's ceremonial tankard filled with three and a half liters of the best Franconian wine. After having drunk and passed the cup among his subordinates, Tilly then, with a touch of humor, offered to spare the town and the lives of the councillors if one of its representatives could empty the tankard in one go. Nusch, a former mayor, who seems to have been good at drinking, agreed to try. He succeeded and saved the town. Apparently he slept for three days after the feat. Five times a day in the marketplace the doors on either side of the clock open and the figures of Tilly and Nusch re-enact the historic drinking feat.

Romantik Hotel Markusturm
Rothenburg

In 1945 the Allies ordered Rothenburg destroyed as part of the war reprisals. An American General, remembering the picture of Rothenburg that hung on his mother's wall, tried to spare the town. His efforts were successful and although Rothenburg was somewhat damaged, the town remained intact.

Rothenburg is a town to be explored on foot - buy a guide that includes a walking tour and set out to explore the town. Be sure to include a section of the city walls: climb the stairs to the walkway and follow the covered ramparts which almost encircle the town.

Rothenburg has many lovely shops and boutiques, one of the most enchanting of which is Kathe Wohlfahrt's Christkindlmarkt. Claiming to offer the world's largest selection of Christmas items, a tiny storefront near the market square opens up to a vast fairyland of decorated Christmas trees and animated Stieff animals.

When it is time to leave Rothenburg you can take an early evening bus departing for WURZBURG, FRANKFURT or HEIDELBERG. Alternately, you can take a local train to WURZBURG and from there make fast rail connections to major German and European cities.

Black Forest

⊙BAD HERRENALB

Baden Baden ★

Höllstrasse

"*Schwarzwald*"

● Freudenstadt

● Lossburg

Wolfach ● Alpirsbach

Hausach ●● Schiltach

Gutach ●

● Freilichtmuseum

Bleibach ●
Gutach ● ⊙ TRIBERG
Waldkirch ●
Glottertal ●● ● Schonwald
St. Peter ● Furtwangen
FREIBURG ⊙ ● St. Margen

● Donaueschingen

Hinterzarten ●

Feldberg ★ ● Titisee
Todtnau ●
T.-Gschwend ● Aha ★ Schluchsee
Schaffhausen ● BUSINGEN
Badenweiler ★ Stein am Rhein ● Mainau
Burgeln ● Weimbach Todtmoos ● Hohenschwand ● Meersburg
Castle Neuenweg ⊙ KONSTANZ
Schwieghof

Switzerland

Bodensee

⊙ *Overnight Stops*
★ *Alternate Hotel Choices*
See Hotel Section of Guide

Hamburg
● Cologne
● Frankfurt
Munich

37

Black Forest

The Black Forest is a delightful mix of dense forests, mountains, spectacular crevasses, wild rivers and quiet valleys.   This is an area of great beauty.   In winter, when quietly blanketed in snow, this is a sportsman's paradise.   In summer too, sports are popular - especially hiking, with 22,000 kilometers of hiking trails in the region. The Black Forest is also gorgeous when the weathered, country farmhouses are set against a landscape of various shades of lush green.   This itinerary follows the peaks and forests of the region.

The people show a strong pride in the cultural tradition of the Black Forest, folk costumes are still worn on Sundays, holidays and at weddings. The dress of the Gutachtal is the best known, featuring billowing black skirts and the Gutach straw hat - a costume which has become a symbol of the region. Unmarried women wear hats adorned with red pom poms, while married women wear more conservative black. Medieval market squares and patrician houses add grandeur and character to the towns and weathered great farmhouses dress the landscape. People come to the Black Forest to rest and use its thermal spas and resorts, and, with health a main focus, fresh food accompanied by fine wines is demanded. Culinary specialties include: trout - fresh from streams, ham - smoked dark and flavorful, fruit brandies - most popular of which is a cherry liqueur known as kirschwasser, internationally recognized wines, and, of course, the ever delicious Schwarzwalder torte mit schlag (Black Forest torte with cream).

If time and energy allow, try hiking without a backpack, a program whereby you set out each morning for a hike of 12 to 17 miles with only a thoughtfully packed lunch to carry, and when you arrive at your next hotel, your luggage will be waiting in your room. There are three packaged routes that are priced to include lodging and two meals. Each routing - "On the Track of the Stag", "Following the Path of the Clock Carriers", and "Around Feldberg" - takes approximately one week with five to seven hours of hiking scheduled for each day. Destination III on this itinerary, the Parkhotel Wehrle in Triberg, is involved in this program.

ORIGINATING CITY   KONSTANZ

Konstanz, on the border of Switzerland and just a short drive from Austria, is a convenient starting point for this itinerary. This itinerary not only ties in very well for the traveler coming from Switzerland or Austria, but also connects beautifully with the "Bavarian Highlights" itinerary in this guide. A hint that this city was once a Roman fortress is hidden in its name - "Konstanz" derives from a Roman, Constantius Chlorus. In Roman times Konstanz had over 80,000 residents. Today Konstanz is still a large city whose surrounding vineyards produce some of Germany's finest wines.

Konstanz is located on Lake Constance or Der Bodensee. On a warm day, consider a boat ride across the lake from Konstanz to Meersburg. This medieval town is certainly one of the loveliest old towns in Europe. Here you find the Alte Schloss: dating from the 7th century, this is the oldest inhabited castle in Germany. You will also see in Meersburg the baroque style Neue Schloss (or new castle) which is really not so new as it was built in the middle of the 18th century.

There is a highly recommended side excursion by boat to the tiny island of Mainau. For garden lovers especially, this will be a real treat. The entire island has been transformed by the owner, a Swedish count, into a tropical paradise. The fragrant gardens bloom from March to October, but are at their peak of glory in May when tulips dominate the gardens and in October when over 20,000 dahlias color the island.

DESTINATION I   BUSINGEN   Alte Rheinmuhle

Travel a short distance by car from Konstanz, winding back and forth along the German-Swiss border to the small and popular village of STEIN AM RHEIN. Colorful frescoes, intricate painted facades, stained glass windows and bright flower boxes and ornate wrought-iron signs dress the main square of this small riverside town. The ROTER OCHSEN, a charming tavern-restaurant, is set on the square and since 1446 has tempted many to linger over a cold, refreshing beer. Allow time to visit the 450-year-old Rathaus (Town Hall) and the 11th-century Benedictine Abbey of St George which harbors a fine small museum, carved woodworkings and paintings.

*Alte Rheinmuhle
Busingen*

From Stein am Rhein the road winds along the Untersee and the Rhine river, a graceful scene of green hills capped by monasteries, castles, citadels and charming villages (Diessenhofen, Gailingen, Obergailingen, Rheinklingen). Continue on to BUSINGEN, a small enclave of German soil, encircled completely by Switzerland. Here you will discover a timbered mill that dates back to 1674. There is nothing more charming than a timbered, heavy beamed mill converted to an inn. The back of the ALTE RHEINMUHLE hugs the edge of the Rhine and from the first floor dining room an entire wall of windows exposes a blissful river scene. The hotel has earned an outstanding reputation for its cuisine and extensive wine cellar. The bedrooms are decorated in a country theme and some are furnished with antiques. Request, if possible, a room overlooking the Rhine. How romantic to enjoy a gourmet dinner in an enchanting restaurant, then to be lulled to sleep by the river flowing beneath your window.

Although in Switzerland, SCHAFFHAUSEN lies only 2 miles west of Busingen and merits a detour.   Constructed upon the site where the busy Rhine river boat traffic was interrupted for portage around the nearby huge waterfall (the Rheinfall), Schaffhausen grew into a very important medieval city.   It was granted a city charter in 1045, joined the Swiss Confederation in 1501, constructed its first hydroelectric works in 1866, and now supports a population of over 40,000. Schaffhausen is an elegant, medieval city that sits dramatically above the impressive Rheinfall.   The old city is a complex of little winding pedestrian streets and passages studded by sidewalk cafes.   It is fun to wander on Vorstadt, a main street where smart shops nestle into the first floors of old houses whose facades are ornately sculpted and painted.   Shadowing the city and river is Munot Fortress, a circular keep constructed between 1564 and 1585.   Uninhabited today, a watchman however continues to ring the old bell each evening, a signal to the revelers of other centuries that the town gate and public houses were soon to close.

A few minutes' drive west of Schaffhausen is the boat station where you board a small skiff that travels out to the base of a single rock that rises in mid-fall.   You climb out of the small boat and clamber up the spray-soaked staircase to stand almost inside the cascade.   Described by Goethe as "the source of the ocean", at 70 feet this is Europe's mightiest waterfall.

From Schaffhausen travel north in the direction of DONAUESHINGEN and then west in the direction of Freiburg and the Black Forest.   At HINTERZARTEN the road descends and winds down into a valley bounded by forest.   The road cuts through narrow, high stone canyon walls: the drive is beautiful.   The next village you come to is FALKENSTEIG followed almost immediately by the town of BUCHENBACH where the densely forested valley opens up again with snow-capped mountains visible in the distance.   En route to Freiburg you will pass the few houses that constitute the village of BURG and then the old barns set on the river's edge at ZEITEN. The road then cuts through a wide valley where residential homes spread out on rolling low hillsides.

Oberkirch's Weinstuben
Freiburg

With a gorgeous setting at the base of the mountains, FREIBURG is a delightful city. The tree-covered hills actually come right down within a block or two of the center of town. Full of character, the old section, founded in 1120, is laden with numerous quaint buildings, and the main square boasts a dramatically beautiful cathedral whose tall spires crest all vistas. Freiburg provides wonderful shopping and a lovely inn: on the church square, at the center of the old city, is OBERKIRCH'S WEINSTUBEN, a cozy wine tavern-hotel combination. This inn is located in two buildings. The principal building sits on the Munsterplatz in the shadow of Freiburg's striking cathedral, the other just a short cobblestone block away. The Weinstuben serves a satisfying lunch or dinner in a very congenial, cozy atmosphere. Beamed ceilings, wooden tables, white linen and contented chatter set the mood for the stuben, a popular choice for dining. The 31 rooms, found either directly above the weinstube or in the neighboring building, are all comfortable and very attractive in a traditional decor. It is somewhat difficult to maneuver by auto through the pedestrian dominated area, especially during the Saturday market, but the hotel provides a map and directions for parking.

DESTINATION III TRIBERG Parkhotel Wehrle

Note: The route suggested from Freiburg to Titisee is a scenic circle trip through the southern region of the Black Forest. Depending on your time frame you can include this journey or head directly north from Freiburg to the country market town of St Margen.

From Freiburg head south in the direction of Basel. This route travels at the base of orchards and vineyards through small villages, with a destination of Badenweiler only 30 kilometers away. STAUFEN is particularly pretty with a colorful market place, interesting Rathaus and castle ruins. BADENWEILER is a sleepy German village near the Swiss border and is one of Germany's oldest spa towns with a history that dates back 2,000 years. The Romans discovered that the waters of Germany had remarkable curative powers and thus was born the German spa. Ever since, "taking the waters" in Germany, by drinking them or bathing in them, has proven a popular formula for those bent on healing, soothing, relaxing or beautifying the body. And because music, art and sports have long been considered as important to the restorative process as their medicinal waters, muds and herbs, the spas have become the meccas for those seeking a vacation that will provide for all the senses. Badenweiler is one of Germany's 250 registered spas, and the comfort of its visitors is the town's primary concern: all streets are closed to traffic after one each afternoon to provide for quiet and calm. This fascinating town has a Kurhaus, or concert hall, that boasts performances three times a day, seminars and tea in the afternoon. The concerts are held either indoors or in a lovely outdoor setting amongst flowers. An old bath house dates back 100 years, but a newly constructed bath house is set in a building of glass and metal with an all-encompassing exposure to the surrounding greenery. Take time to find a wonderful inn, the ROMANTIK HOTEL SONNE, and its owner, Herr Fischer. If time permits, linger here, as this hotel boasts as much tradition as the town and Herr Fischer is an exceptional host and maintains the excellence of service that previous generations of his family have established.

Note: An excursion just 12 miles south will take you to BURGELN CASTLE. Set on an extension of the Blauen, it provides an impressive view of the surrounding countryside as far as the Swiss Alps.

From Badenweiler continue east in the direction of SCHONAU IM SCHWARZWALD. You come first to the town of SCHWIEGHOF, located at the base of the mountains, then the road winds and loops up through small farming villages. After NEUENWEG the road reaches the top of the summit and vistas open to rolling hills settled below. The drive then curves down, banked on one side by rocky cliffs and on the other side by green slopes. Hiking trails beckon in every direction. WEMBACH is a pretty village of weathered farmhouses and wooden stables with ski lifts dotting the edge of town.

A few miles farther and you arrive at the town of T.-GSCHWEND. From here you can either continue north through the resort towns of TODTNAU, FELDBERG (nice view from the town's chairlift), on to TITISEE, or detour a little longer by winding south in the direction of TODTMOOS. GESCHWEND is a pretty village edged by farmhouses and topped by the steeple of its church. A lovely old lumber mill maintains a picturesque setting on the water's edge. PRAG is a sweet hamlet tucked into the valley and cut by a rushing stream.

Todtmoos is a resort town whose setting is softened in winter by layers of snow. Ski lifts sit right on the edge of town. Soon after Todtmoos is the elegant spa town of HOCHENSCHWAND where you follow the Scharza river north in the direction of Schluchsee. SCHLUCHSEE is a lovely large lake, its shores unspoilt by development. At the town of AHA heavy forests line the road as it climbs up and then winds down to another lake and quiet valley. Titisee is a pretty little village on the banks of the lake with the same name, where the timberline comes right down to the water's edge, hiding a number of chalets nestled along the shores.

From Titisee travel a few miles north to the junction of the main road then head west in the direction of Freiburg for a few miles before veering north again to the country market town of ST MARGEN. Set on a high plateau, the town boasts a baroque church. A few miles farther on is the resort town of ST PETER whose abbey towers dominate the skyline. From St Peter the road twists and winds along the river and reaches a crest at KANDEL. If you want to stretch your legs, note that it is about a fifteen-minute walk along the road to the pavilion for a view of the entire region. The panorama displays the Vosges mountains in France to the Rhine plain and the towers of St Peter's Abbey and the Feldberg and Belchen heights in the Black Forest.

The road curls down from Kandel to the charming town of Glotteral. Just outside GLOTTERAL take the main road north in the direction of Freudenstadt. WALDKIRCH is a larger town with a pretty setting and a market place adorned by some 18th-century houses. Beyond the town of GUTACH you come to BLEIBACH where you turn in the direction of Furtwangen. Before leaving Bleibach, allow yourself to be tempted to stop for a meal at the HOTEL STOLLEN. Set on a corner of the main street, this charming timbered building has an excellent restaurant where even a simple request of soup and salad can prove to be a gourmet's delight, graciously served and beautifully presented. From Bleibach the road curves once more back along the base of the Black Forest through the villages of SIMONWALD and OBERSIMONWALD, then climbs to GUTENBACH and on to FURTWANGEN.

Not long after leaving Furtwangen you arrive at SCHONWALD, a small town whose history deserves mention. This is where the cuckoo clock was born.

Schonwald was the home of Franz Anton Ketterer who at the beginning of the 18th century thought of combining a clock with bellows. He incorporated a timepiece with a cuckoo carved in wood whose tiny bellows marked the hours with the notes of a cuckoo call. Records show that clocks were manufactured in the Black Forest as early as 1630, but when cuckoo clocks were invented, they became the rage. The original clocks were constructed entirely out of wood, from their inner works to wheels, while the more expensive specimens had glass bells that struck the hours. The dials with the traditional Roman numerals were painted and decorated with all sorts of colorful designs - flower wreaths, angels and peasant scenes. With winter snows and cold keeping families indoors, it was not unusual to find all members of the peasant households working on the clocks. Even now clock-making is a considerable industry for the region, and, although factories exist, the production of cuckoo clocks is still frequently a home business with the whole family working on the intricately carved boxes and painted dials.

TRIBERG, located in the heart of the Black Forest just a few miles beyond Schonwald, is an ideal spot to stay. The town has one main street comprised of clock shop after clock shop whose selection, variety and competitive prices will amaze you. Catering to tourists, they are all equipped to accept major credit cards and see that your clocks are shipped safely to the destination of your choice. At the town's edge is a romantic waterfall and local Black Forest Museum whose walls are covered in a display of clocks, crafts, regional costumes and a mineral exhibit. Tour buses will come and go from Triberg in the course of a day but overnighting here affords you the luxury of an evening to think about and select a clock for your home. The PARKHOTEL WEHRLE, located in an ivy-covered yellow stone building, occupies a corner position on the main street. For those of you who are fortunate enough to have the Wehrle as a base for your travels, you will experience the professional care and welcome of Herr and Frau Claus Blum, the warmth of their hotel and the excellence of their restaurant.

The Parkhotel Wehrle, in conjunction with a number of other regional hotels, has organized walking vacations where your luggage is sent ahead to the next hotel.

Walking is a wonderful way to see the region. The hotel can provide you with details on the program.

Parkhotel Wehrle
Triberg

DESTINATION IV   **BAD HERRENALB**   Monch's Posthotel

From Triberg continue on route 33 in the direction of Offenburg. The countryside is very lush, dotted by farmhouses typical of the region. Approximately a half-hour's drive from Triberg brings you to a complex of farmhouses, clustered together as architectural examples of what the farm life was like in the "olden days". Located near the town of GUTACH, this marvelous outdoor museum with the fancy name of Bogtsbauernhof Schwarzwaelder Freilichtmuseum is well worth a visit.

After leaving the museum, just before the town of HAUSSACH, follow signs to Freudenstadt then travel a valley cut by the scenic Gutach river. At WOLFACH pass through the town's gates, follow the attractive main street, cross the Gutach and then turn right following signs again to Freudenstadt. The road winds back into the hills, following the river. Along the way you will see many wonderful Black Forest farmhouses. Next you come to the picturesque town of SHILTACH with its wooden gabled houses. From Schiltach the road climbs and the "Schwarzwald Hochstrasse" (or High Road of the Black Forest) officially begins. The route takes you through the town of ALPIRSBACH, a fairly large town whose Romanesque cloister and timbered facades still dominate its older section. The road then twists up through the trees to the fairly modern town of LOSSBURG and then on to FREUDENSTADT. Destroyed by fire in 1945, Freudenstadt is a modern resort town whose large castle square is interesting in that it was laid out in the 16th century for a castle that was never built.

Enjoy the heavily forested highroad of the Black Forest as it loops down to one of Europe's most elegant and renowned spa towns, BADEN-BADEN. Manicured gardens, white wrought-iron lounge chairs set out to take full advantage of the sun, cobbled pedestrian streets, exclusive boutiques, antique shops, parks, fountains and an abundance of colorful flowers stage a delightfully romantic setting in this beautiful city. Open to the Rhine Plains, but protected from harsh winds by the surrounding hills, Baden-Baden enjoys a unique climate and her loyal patrons return year after year, swearing to the curative powers of the climate and the waters.

Spring comes early and the parks and gardens are a mass of blossoms, summer is long and sunny, autumn colors the foliage on the Lichtentaler Allee in russet hues, and winter is mild and beautiful with the surrounding mountains dusted in powdery snow. With its temperate climate, medicinal springs and gorgeous setting, Baden-

Baden has been popular since Roman times. It possesses one of the world's finest botanical gardens: set along the banks of the River Oos, the open English-type gardens and parkland afford serene paths that loop around the Kurhaus, Trinkhalle and Casino. During the warmer months, concerts are held at the Kurhaus, the focal point of social activity and entertainment. An exclusive meeting place, the Casino, built in the middle of the 19th century, is furnished in the elegant style of the French Renaissance.

Closed to traffic, the Old Town, nestled below the collegiate church, is a wonderful place for shopping. The stores display their elegant wares artistically, ever competing with the smells from the nearby pastry shops which summon you to an afternoon tea break. Baden-Baden is also a sportsman's paradise - golf, riding, tennis, fishing and hiking are all available in the vicinity. Race week is held each year in August when Baden-Baden becomes a sophisticated meeting place for the wealthy "horsy set". One of the town's traditional attractions is the Merkur mountain railway. Built in 1913, it reopened after repairs in the spring of 1979 and you can now travel up the incline and enjoy sweeping vistas from the observation tower at its summit.

Note: Baden-Baden is a delightful, romantic city and would serve as a lovely base, especially if you would like to rest and take advantage of the spa facilities. The HOTEL ZUM HIRSCH, located in the pedestrian section of the Old Town, is recommended should you decide to stay.

After a shopping spree and perhaps a snack in Baden-Baden at one of its tempting coffee or pastry shops, continue on for about half an hour to BAD HERRENALB, a smaller spa town tucked away in the forested hills. Here you will find the beautiful MONCH'S POSTHOTEL. This post hotel carries the name of the family that has managed it since 1863. Monch's Posthotel exudes elegance and olde worlde charm. Girls dressed in dirndls greet you as you arrive. Through a small arched wooden doorway, in the oldest part of the building, is a delightful restaurant where dark wooden booths and tables contrast richly with the blue tiles, freshly pressed curtains and grey-blue linens. Off the entry is a larger, more formal dining room. In summer breakfast is served in the garden. The beautiful bedrooms are decorated in warm colors, patterned fabrics and traditional furnishings. An added bonus is the outdoor swimming pool attractively set in the garden. Huddled deep in a lavishly wooded intersection of seven valleys, Bad Herrenalb is an ideal spot to end your Black Forest excursion and the Monch's Posthotel will prove a highlight of your trip.

Monch's Posthotel
Bad Herrenalb

Black Forest

Exploring the Rhine and Moselle

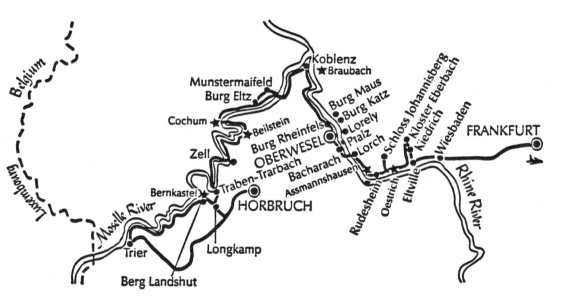

◉ Overnight Stops
★ Alternate Hotel Choices
   See Hotel Section of Guide ✈ Airport

Exploring the Rhine and Moselle

The magical River Rhine is a magnet for visitors drawn by tales of its majesty and beauty. This itinerary covers two of its loveliest areas - the Rheingau wine region and the famous Rhine gorge. Powerful and broad, the River Rhine rushes towards the sea. High above the river, castles guard the heights or lie on islands amidst the churning flow. The river narrows to swirl past the legendary Lorelei rock whose muse dashed unwary sailors and their boats onto jagged rocks. A procession of famous villages and towns hug the river's banks. At Koblenz "Father Rhine" is joined by his loveliest daughter, the Moselle river. The Moselle's path is gentler, looping lazily back and forth as it passes tiny ribbon villages of half-timbered houses. Steep vineyards line her banks while castles stand guard from the hilltops above. The beauty of these rivers is enough to fill a rich chapter in your vacation, but if this is not sufficient to tempt you, be reminded that this itinerary offers the opportunity to alternate excursions with sampling the fine wines of the Rheingau, Mittelrhein and Moselle wine regions.

Beilstein on the Moselle River

ORIGINATING CITY   FRANKFURT

Frankfurt is a convenient starting point to begin an itinerary. Frankfurt airport, Rhein Main, is the destination of planes from all over the world. Centuries of flourishing commerce have brought this city great prosperity: its commercial importance led to it being a target for wave after wave of Allied bombers during World War II. Those responsible for reconstruction after the war chose to rebuild Frankfurt as a modern city. Fortunately a few historic gems have been restored: Goethe House, where Johann Wolfgang von Goethe was born in 1749, is open as a museum showing how a well-to-do family lived in the 18th century, and nearby you find the Romerberg - a square of old restored gabled buildings. Today, Frankfurt's prosperity lives on in streets of elegant shops, attractive restaurants, its vast entertainment calendar and its large conventions or fairs. As in days of old, it is here that the roads converge, but nowadays it is the trains, planes and autobahns that whisk you to all parts of Germany.

If you arrive at Frankfurt airport late in the day after a long transatlantic flight and are anxious to begin rural explorations, you will be pleased to note that the Romantik Hotel Schwan in Oestrich-Winkel is only a 45-minute drive from the Frankfurt airport.

DESTINATION I   OBERWESEL   Auf Schonburg

Follow the autobahn 66 west from FRANKFURT through WIESBADEN. In a few miles the autobahn ends and continues as road 42: this main road and the busy inter-city railway trace the river's bank. The first part of today's itinerary loops back and forth from this main artery, exploring the gently sloping vineyard-covered hillsides that line the bank of the River Rhine. Known as the "Rheingau", this small wine area is especially famous for its Riesling wines.

A short drive brings you to the wine town of ELTVILLE where in medieval times the archbishops of Mainz had their summer palaces. Here you leave the busy river road and climb through the vineyards to KIEDRICH. Drive into the little village and visit its pretty pink church with its elaborate interior before continuing up the hill to KLOSTER EBERBACH. Set in a snug little hollow at the upper reaches of the vineyards, this former Cistercian monastery enjoyed 700 years of prosperity thanks to the production of wine. The Cistercian monks led an austere, silent life of prayer and hard work, allotting only a few hours a night for sleep on hard, narrow wooden pallets. Stroll through the quiet cloisters and cool halls with their graceful fan-vaulted ceilings to the refectory which now houses an impressive collection of enormous old wine presses. The severe architecture, plain plaster walls and lack of embellishments mirror the austere lifestyle led by the monks.

Leaving the monastery grounds, turn to the right and follow the country road as it dips down through the vineyards back to the river at HATTENHEIM. Drive through the old town center to the adjacent village of OESTRICH. Turn left down one of the winding village streets and you emerge back on the busy Rhineside road for the short drive to WINKEL.

Turn right in Winkel and follow the road up through the vineyards to the bright yellow castle on the hill, the SCHLOSS JOHANNISBERG. This famous castle is the emblem of wines produced in this area and its name, "Johannisberg", is synonymous with the production of Riesling wine. While you cannot go inside the castle, you can sample wines in the tasting room or savor wine with a bite of lunch in the terrace restaurant. On a fine day the castle terrace affords a panoramic view across the vineyards to the river below.

Note: The palace cellars contain century-old wines of fabulous value. You can arrange for a private tour of the cellars, on weekdays only, by writing to Herr

Gundert, Schloss Johannisberg, 6222 Geisenheim-Johannisberg.

Returning to the river road, it is a short distance to the most famous wine town of this area, RUDESHEIM.   Park you car by the river, bypass the many tourist shops selling gaudy souvenirs and head for the town's most picturesque street, Drosselgrasse.   Here, on what is reputed to be the jolliest street in the world, one wine tavern props up another.   Even if you do not partake of the wine, it is fun to wander along this festive street.   A short stroll along the river brings you to the more serious side of wine production, the wine museum in Bromserburg Castle. This splendid museum is filled with artifacts pertaining to the production of wine from the earliest days.

Leaving Rudesheim, the river road winds below steeply terraced vineyards as the river Rhine forsakes its gently sloping banks and turns north into a rocky gorge. Passing below the ruins of EHRENFELS CASTLE, the MAUSETURM (Mouse Tower) comes into view on an island near the opposite bank.   Legend has it that Archbishop Hatto II was a cruel master who paid a terrible price for his sins: he was driven into the mouse tower by mice who then proceeded to eat him alive.

The river valley narrows as you near the town of ASSMANNSHAUSEN and the first of the famous castles that overlook the river comes into view on the opposite bank - RHEINSTEIN CASTLE.   Take time to drive into Assmannshausen, and explore its poky narrow streets full of charming little old houses.   The wisteria-covered terrace of the HOTEL KRONE provides you with a refreshment stop and fine views of the passing river life.

As you drive north along the riverbank, as fast as one castle disappears from view, another comes into sight perched high above the rocky river valley.   The Rheingau wine region ends in the little town of LORCH, where you take the small chugging car ferry that fights the strong river currents and slowly transports you across the river to RHEINDIEBACH.   As you enter the Mittelrhein wine district, you see the Rheingau's verdant vineyards gently sloping to the river replaced by steep river terraces occupying every southern facing slope, where the grapes can soak up the warm summer sun. Between the vineyards, the high river banks are thickly wooded.

It is just a few minutes' drive from the ferry to BACHARACH. Park your car by the river and walk into the town to discover that the plain riverfront facade conceals a picturesque village of half-timbered medieval houses around a market square. As you leave Bacharach, a much photographed castle, the PFALZ, comes into view marooned on an island amidst the swirling flow.

As you drive into OBERWESEL, pause at the foot of the castle road and visit the reddish-pink church, the Liebfrauenkirche. Gothic in style, the church is noted for its many beautiful altarpieces, the oldest built in 1506. In the surrounding vineyards you will find Oberwesel, a delightful unpretentious wine town.

Tonight's prize, the AUF SCHONBURG castle, comes into view high above the town. Turn left by the church and follow the winding road upwards to the castle. Cross the wooden bridge spanning the gully that isolates the Auf Schonburg on its rocky bluff. Park your car beneath the castle walls and climb the well-worn cobbles that wind you through the castle to the hotel at the summit. The facade is out of a fairytale - towers, turrets, battlements and a dear little black and white building tucked against the outer castle wall. The interior is a joy - little bedrooms nestled in a circular tower or tucked neatly into nooks in the old buildings, romantic old beds and furnishings. (Incidentally some of the castle's most romantic rooms do not have Rhine river views.) Wonderful food is served in cozy dining rooms with service that could not be kinder. And the view! From the hotel a magnificent landscape spreads before you as the hillside drops steeply to the village and the swiftly flowing river. Let the enchantment of your castle hotel tempt you to stay for several days, giving you time to explore the castles that you have seen from a distance, time for a leisurely river "cruise" and time to visit the secluded little villages high above the river valley.

A thousand years ago your hotel, the Auf Schonburg, was built as a Roman fortress. It played its part in the centuries of European history until it was almost destroyed by the French in 1689. For over 200 years it lay in ruins until a wealthy New York banker, whose family emigrated from these parts, bought the property and spent 35 years and two million gold marks on restoring the castle as a summer home. In 1951 his son sold the castle back to the town which converted a portion into a youth hostel. Several years later Hans Huttl, an enterprising local vintner, converted another portion into this exquisite hotel.

Auf Schonburg
Oberwesel

DESTINATION II   HORBRUCH   Hotel Historische Bergmuhle

As you bid your castle on the Rhine farewell, glance to the river where it swirls and eddies amongst the rocks on the opposite bank. Legend has it that these rocks are the seven maidens of Oberwesel Castle who were so cold-hearted towards their suitors that the river overturned their boat and turned them into stone.

Around the first river bend, the fabled LORELEI rock comes into view. The currents around the rock, which juts out sharply into the river, are so dangerous that the legend arose of an enchantress sitting high atop the rock combing her golden tresses and so entrancing the sailors with her singing that the rules of navigation were forgotten and their boats were dashed onto the rocks.

The Rhine landscape is splendid when viewed from the river but even finer views await you from the ramparts of the castle, BURG RHEINFELS, located high above ST GOAR. Below flows the mighty Rhine dotted with chugging barges and on the opposite bank are the whimsically named BURG MAUZ (Mouse Castle) and the adjacent larger BURG KATZ (Cat Castle). In the Burg Rheinfels museum, a model shows that what is now largely a ruin, was once a mighty fortress.

Keeping the river close company, about a 45-minute drive brings you to the outskirts of KOBLENZ where you bid the River Rhine farewell and by following signposts for TRIER, navigate through town to the banks of the MOSELLE RIVER.

The pageant of the river bank marches steadily on, but how different the Moselle is to the Rhine. The Moselle is narrower, moving more slowly -   gracefully looping back and forth. The road too is narrower, with thankfully less traffic and no busy adjacent railway track. The Moselle's steep banks are uniformly covered with vines - for this is wine country. Every little ribbon village, with the terraced vineyards rising steeply behind it, is involved in the production of wine. The villages are often no more than a cluster of houses, yet they all have their own famous brand of wine.

High above the river, castles guard the heights. The loveliest and best preserved castle, the BURG ELTZ, is most easily reached by taking one of the many bridges

Exploring the Rhine and Moselle

to the river's northern bank and following the riverside road to the tiny hamlet of HATZENPORT. Turn right in the village for the short drive to MUNSTERMAIFELD and on to WIERSCHEM, following signposts for your destination, the Burg Eltz. You will soon see an area designated for parking. Leave your car here (no cars allowed at the castle) and follow the well marked paths to Burg Eltz. Your trail winds through a beautiful forest where benches are strategically placed should you need to rest or just pause to see the view. You might think you are on the wrong path because you walk for about fifteen minutes before catching your first glimpse of the majestic turreted castle in a clearing of the woods. Tour the rooms furnished in Gothic style and admire the collections of armor and weapons.

Retrace your path back to your car, then drive down the hill to the Moselle river and follow the road that hugs the northern bank for the short drive into COCHEM. Park your car and explore the pedestrian center of this small town. Turn a blind eye to the rather tacky souvenir shops and let yourself be tempted inside a coffee shop for some mouthwatering pastries and a cup of coffee. Thus fortified, wander through the narrow streets and follow the well-signposted walk to the castle, REICHSBURG COCHEM, sitting atop a hill above the town. The trek is worth it, for while the valley is beautiful when viewed from below, the view from above is spectacular.

As you leave Cochem, the prettiest stretch of the Moselle opens up before you as the loops of the river almost double back on themselves. Cross the river at Cochem and follow the river to BEILSTEIN. The village is perfect - a tiny cobbled square crowded by centuries-old houses. Walk up the quiet cobbled streets to the church and return to the square to sample wine in the cool deep cellars of the HAUS LIPMANN. Or, if the weather is warm, settle on the hotel's terrace to watch the little ferry as it shuttles cars back and forth across the river while long river barges chug slowly by.

Continuing along the winding river course, you see vineyards rising steeper and steeper until you wonder just how the vintners reach them to cultivate their crops. These are amongst the steepest vineyards in the world. At ZELL they rise immediately behind the narrow town.

Several more long looping bends and you come to the twin villages of TRABEN-TRARBACH. Leave the river behind and take the small road in the center of Trarbach that winds you upwards out of the river valley to LONGKAMP. Turn left in the center of Longkamp following signs for the road 327 to KOBLENZ. Turn left on 327 towards Koblenz, then it is only a few miles to the RHAUNEN exit. You will find the HISTORISCHE BERGMUHLE a short drive from the junction, about half a mile beyond the pastoral village of HORBRUCH.

It is a little complicated getting to the hotel - a detailed map will certainly aid you - but the effort is worthwhile for the Historische Bergmuhle is one of those rare "perfect hideaways" - an idyllic old mill, the wheel still turning lazily beyond the dining room window. Bedrooms in the old mill are named after country animals and, apart from being beautifully decorated, are stocked with thoughtful little extras that make a stay memorable - proper sewing kits, hair spray and perfume. The four new rooms in the granary are equally as lovely in their decor. Rudiger and Anneliese Liller are your charming hosts: their hotel looks so charming because Anneliese Liller is a creative interior decorator.

A little corner room is named in honor of Napoleon, for the mill has associations with this famous soldier. The story goes that in 1804 Napoleon was camped in a nearby town, and, needing to raise money to continue his campaign, he sold the buildings in the village. The mill was purchased by the enterprising Peter Lietzenburger who had the foresight to realise that once Napoleon left, the old owner would reclaim his property. To guard against this happening, he had the mill taken apart stone by stone and erected 25 kilometers away in this quiet green valley outside the village of Horbruch.

Hotel Historische Bergmuhle
Horbruch

Plan on spending several days in your hideaway above the Moselle river valley, taking daytrips to the Moselle and the surrounding countryside.

A suggestion for a daytrip is to retrace your path to Longkamp and follow signs for BERNKASTEL-KUES. The road drops steeply as it enters the Moselle river valley. Before you enter the town, look for a small sign directing you to the BERG LANDSHUT, an impressive ruined castle above the town. From the castle grounds, the vineyards tumble steeply to the river below and the view is spectacular.

Bernkastel-Kues is two towns, with Kues lying across the river. In this wine valley Bernkastel stands out as being the most attractive larger town. Park your car by the river and explore the old town where colorful 400-year-old half-timbered houses are grouped around a lovely marketplace. In July and August a long leisurely cruise takes you roundtrip from Bernkastel to Trier. The boat leaves from in front of the town at 9:30 AM arriving in Trier at 1:45 PM. With the afternoon free to explore Trier, you arrive back at Bernkastel at 8:30 PM. (Note: Timetables change, so please verify boat information with the Hans Michels Boat Company, 5550 Bernkastel-Kues, telephone 06531-6897.)

An alternative to the boat trip to Trier is to drive, which takes about an hour following the road along the river. Founded by the Roman Emperor Augustus in 15 BC, TRIER had the largest fortified gateway in the Roman Empire, the Porta Nigra. Still intact, it stands guard over the city limits nearly twenty centuries later. This gate is like a giant wedding cake of three and a half tiers standing nearly a hundred feet high.

The tourist office by the Porta Nigra will supply you with a city map showing you the route to the Roman amphitheater and a map of the walk through the vineyards. The amphitheater was built above the town to provide up to 20,000 people with gladiatorial entertainment. After the Roman Empire fell, the site was used as a quarry, and now soft grassy mounds have taken the place of the stone seats and now from behind the amphitheater, the Weinlehrpfad, an educational wine path, leads you up through the vineyards.

Don't leave Trier without also going to the center of this small city where you will find an extremely colorful large plaza with beautiful medieval houses extending for several blocks.

When your sightseeing in Trier is complete, follow signs for autobahn 1 south towards SAARBRUCKEN. After about 15 miles, turn north on road 327 signposted for Koblenz. The scenery is lovely - rolling fields of waving wheat and large meadowlands, a beautiful contrast to the sunburned vineyards of the Moselle valley. About an hour's drive brings you to familiar scenery as you return to Horbruch and the Historische Bergmuhle.

When it is time to leave Horbruch, it is only a short drive to Germany's borders with Luxembourg, France and Belgium. Of course you can return to Frankfurt to tie in with another German itinerary.

Exploring the Rhine and Moselle

The Romantic Road
and The Neckar Valley

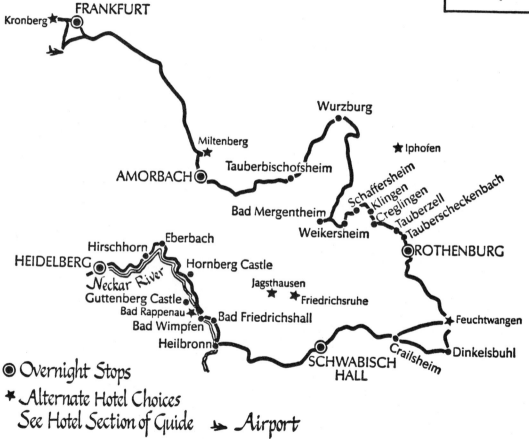

Hamburg

Cologne

Frankfurt
Munich

FRANKFURT

Kronberg

Wurzburg

Miltenberg

Iphofen

Tauberbischofsheim

AMORBACH

Schaffersheim
Klingen
Creglingen

Bad Mergentheim

Tauberzell
Tauberscheckenbach

Weikersheim

ROTHENBURG

Eberbach

Hirschhorn

HEIDELBERG

Hornberg Castle

Neckar River

Jagsthausen

Guttenberg Castle

Friedrichsruhe

Bad Rappenau

Bad Friedrichshall

Bad Wimpfen

Feuchtwangen

Heilbronn

Crailsheim

Dinkelsbuhl

SCHWABISCH
HALL

◉ Overnight Stops

★ Alternate Hotel Choices
   See Hotel Section of Guide   ✈ Airport

67

The Romantic Road and The Neckar Valley

The Romantic Road (or Romantische Strasse) is one of Germany's most famous tourist routes - a road that travels between the towns of Wurzburg in Franconia and Fussen in the Bavarian Alps. Every bend along the way between Wurzburg and Rothenburg is spectacular. However, the beauty of the scenery begins to wane a little after leaving Rothenburg, so this itinerary deviates from the traditional route. Rather than traveling the entire 210-mile stretch of the Romantic Road, this itinerary assumes Frankfurt as your arrival city, samples the northern highlights of Germany's most traveled route and then detours west at Rothenberg to incorporate the enchanting city of Schwabisch Hall and the picturesque university city of Heidelberg. However, the beautiful southern portion of the Romantic Road has not been forgotten - it is incorporated into the Bavarian Highlights itinerary.

Rothenburg on the Romantic Road

ORIGINATING CITY FRANKFURT

If you arrive at Frankfurt airport on an international flight, you might be pleased to note that within a half hour's drive is a very stately and luxurious hotel, the Schloss Hotel Kronberg, an idyllic place to rest and be pampered while overcoming jet lag. The Schloss Hotel Kronberg has been offering rooms to guests for over fifty years. Before being converted to a hotel, it served for ten years as a casino for the American military and before that it was a private residence. Once a gathering place for European royalty and many of the ruling monarchs, the hotel has a number of grand halls, stately public rooms, elegant dining rooms and beautiful, expensive accommodations. Its very dignified guest list suggests the understated elegance and sophistication of this luxury hotel.

DESTINATION I AMORBACH Der Schafhof

If you are eager to experience the flavor of the German countryside, it is just a few hours' drive south of the Frankfurt airport to the village of MILTENBERG. Located on the left bend of the Main river, this village is wonderful to explore and a perfect stopping point to stretch your legs. One of the first things you'll notice is a turreted bridge and the fading ruins of a castle on the hillside. The village is a charming mix of cobblestoned streets and sloping slate and tile roofs. It is a quick and rewarding hike up from the market place to the castle ruins for a splendid view overlooking this picturesque village. On Haupstrasse, a street reserved for pedestrians, you will enjoy a number of quaint shops and might choose to sit a while and sample your first "bier und wurst". Miltenberg has an inn, HOTEL ZUM RIESEN, but for one of Germany's most enchanting inns and a guaranteed night of quiet, continue on to the farming village of AMORBACH and DER SCHAFHOF.

A short drive from the center of the village, nestled on a hillside dotted with grazing sheep, you will find your hotel, Der Schafhof.   Built in 1721, it originally belonged to the estate of the Amorbach Benedictine Abbey.   Now the flag bearing the crest of the Winkler family from the Oberhessen district, who held the position of titled millers, is proudly raised in front.   Dr Winkler is an attorney in Oftenbath but still finds time to manage Der Schafhof, still an operating farm with sheep, some goats, hens and ducks.   The family provide excellent accommodations and cuisine.   The decor is consistently beautiful, with a theme of natural dyes and colors of rich browns, soft creams and whites - enriched by the country feeling of weathered beams.   Anyone would feel fortunate for just one night here and envious of those with an extended stay.

Der Schafhof
Amorbach

TAUBERBISCHHOFSHEIM is an appealing small medieval town that you will want to visit en route to Wurzburg. With unspoilt countryside surrounding it, Tauberbischhofsheim has a local history museum housed in the former palace of the Prince Electors of Mainz and a number of interesting churches. Also, the town has recently become a popular center for fencing enthusiasts.

As described back in the 12th century by the well-traveled diplomat, Gottfried von Viterbo, WURZBURG is "lovely, like a rose set in deep-green foliage .. sculpted into the valley like an earthly paradise". This beautiful baroque town is crested by the Marienberg citadel and has at its feet, spanning the river Main, the old bridge lined by statues of saints. Adding to the beauty of the region, vineyards slope down to surround this old university town. Masterpieces of European structure are the Cathedral of St Kilian and the Residenz (the former palace of the prince-bishops). The historic Ratskeller, once the town hall, is now open to the public - a maze of rooms including a witch's hole and large Bierstube. The Marienberg Fortress houses the Mainfrankisches Museum and displays some wonderful treasures including thumbnail sketches by Tiepolo and incredibly beautiful wood carvings by Riemenschneider. Wurzburg is graced with many art treasures and a lovely location on the banks of the looping Main river. The city tempts visitors with its grand wine, beer and local "Meefischli" (Main fish).

Head south from Wurzburg along a country road (19) to BAD MERGENTHEIM on the River Tauber. The old order of the Teutonic Knights left Prussia to reside here in a castle in 1525 and remained until they were disbanded in 1809. The magnificent Renaissance palace now houses a museum on the Teutonic Order as well as a local-history museum. Bad Mergentheim's history as a world renowned health spa dates back to 1826 when a shepherd uncovered an old, long-buried mineral spring.

From Bad Mergentheim, the Romantic Road winds its way along the most scenic stretch of the Tauber valley. The serenity of the lush, ever-changing landscapes in the next few miles epitomizes the meaning of the title given to this idyllic stretch of countryside - the Romantic Road.

The village of WEIKERSHEIM is set on the left bank of the Tauber only a few miles from Bad Mergentheim. The palace of Weikersheim was the former residence and ancestral seat of the Princes of Hohenlohe. The well-preserved interior furnishings of the palace reflect Renaissance, baroque and rococo styles and the baroque gardens are among the finest in Germany.

A short distance farther, pretty half-timbered houses line the market square of ROTTINGEN. This wine center also boasts a castle steeped in legend - Brattenstein Castle.

Your road follows the Tauber as it weaves south, passing under the clock tower building in SCHAFFERSHEIM, through the pretty village of KLINGEN (dominated by its high church steeple), then it winds on to CREGLINGEN with its wealth of romantic vistas and charming houses. People come to Creglingen from all over the world to see the isolated Herrgottskirche which was built about a mile from this medieval city in 1389. Its altarpiece, "Ascension of Mary", dates from 1510 and is a masterful example of the wood carver Tilman Riemenschneider's work and talent. This lovely church stood hidden and forgotten from 1530 to 1832 and miraculously escaped the destruction of World War II.

The road now follows the gentle Tauber as it winds through a narrow lush valley. Quaint villages fill the gaps along the road and the river meanders in their shadow. Footpaths stretch out for miles paralleling this incredibly scenic drive and tempt one to abandon the car and continue the journey by bike or on foot. Along the way you will pass through TAUBERZELL (a farming village with a cluster of timbered houses), TAUBERSCHECKENBACH (a neighboring, equally attractive hamlet), and BETTWAR (with an especially picturesque setting). From Bettwar you can see the medieval "fairytale" town of Rothenburg in the near distance.

ROTHENBURG is an unspoiled gem of the Middle Ages. The outlines of today's existing structure of fortified towers and walls remain intact and date from 1274 when Emperor Rudolf I of Hapsburg proclaimed Rothenburg a free imperial city. It then obtained a charter and the right to self-government, thus becoming responsible solely to the emperor. Remarkably well-preserved from the 14th and 15th centuries, Rothenburg is truly a treasure for all to visit and experience. Its beautiful gates, towers and massive walls stage a stunning silhouette. Stroll the narrow cobbled streets of this little township. Horse drawn carts add to the character of the streets and the clomping of hoofs on cobblestone lends a bit of nostalgia to the activity and bustle. Intricate wrought iron hallmarks and gorgeous displays of flowers decorate many of the facades of the medieval and Renaissance houses. Wander and enjoy the fascination and intriguing personality of each street and alleyway, but be sure to watch the time so that you will not miss the clock chimes in the dramatic town hall.

You will definitely also want to include in your exploring the vast cathedral and other notable structures such as the Poenlein, St Mark's Tower, the White Tower, Gerlach's Forge, the Franciscan Church and the Dominican Convent. Two miles of stone wall with forty towers and gates encircle Rothenburg and you can walk along the ramparts for almost the entire distance. From the municipal gardens on the promontory where Rothenburg was founded, there is a magnificent panoramic view of the town and the surrounding valley. All of Rothenburg has been declared a national monument and its buildings are protected by law. The history of Rothenburg is recreated in pageants and festivals numerous times during the year.

Stay in Rothenburg for as long as your travel arrangements allow: a day is not enough to absorb the history and magic of this delightful medieval town. One must also take the luxury of an afternoon break to sample the town's specialty, Schneeballen (snowballs), a dessert that is a layer of thin strips of pastry rolled up, deep fried and then dusted with confectioner's sugar, its final appearance being that of a snowball: it is utterly delicious.

ADAM DAS KLEINE HOTEL is located near Burg Gasse on a side alley off Herrngasse, Rothenburg's widest street. A small inn favored by many who have come to know, understand and love the temperament of its owner and namesake, Herr Adam. Herr Adam is your host as well as chef and will prepare his version of a gastronomic meal and will delight in your culinary compliments. The bedrooms, a mix of cherished tidbits and lovely furnishings, are found up a steep, narrow, winding stairway. This small hotel enjoys a delightful, quiet location and from many of the rooms you can enjoy views out through lead paned windows onto the castle gardens.

Adam Das Kleine Hotel
Rothenburg

It is disappointing to compare the character of Rothenburg to almost any other medieval town in Europe. Few can challenge its dramatic structures and atmosphere. But don't make the mistake of ending your vacation after your visit to Rothenburg as there are still destinations on this itinerary to pique and satisfy your interests.

The Romantic Road travels south from Rothenburg - shaded by groves of pine trees as it winds through numerous small farming villages. The drive exposes a slice of rural lifestyle as it edges close to farmhouses and open barns. The farmland is rich and green and the orange tile roofs of the village houses provide a lovely contrast. En route is FEUCHTWANGEN, a small town whose market square is referred to as "Franconia's festival hall". Of interest are the Romanesque cloisters, the collegiate church, the Wolgemut altar, St John's Church, historic burgher houses, craft workshops and a local-history museum. The town also has one of the region's most delightful inns - the ROMANTIK HOTEL GREIFEN POST, managed by the Lorentz family. You might choose to use this hotel as your base or simply sample the bounties of its restaurant.

South of Feuchtwangen is the historic old town of DINKELSBUHL, well preserved behind a wall with twenty towers and gateways, which has one main street of picturesque old burgher houses and tourist shops. Its major attraction, however, is the "Kinderzeche" (children's festival), held each year in mid-July to commemorate the town's salvation by the village's brave children in the Thirty Years' War. Consider a short detour south to see Dinkelsbuhl.

Your next stop is SCHWABISCH HALL, a town removed from the ever popular Romantische Strasse by only a short drive through gentle farmland and sleepy villages. Schwabisch Hall profits from the fact that it is not very heavily visited by tourists and therefore has retained much of its original atmosphere, character and charm. Set on two sides of the river, the town boasts picturesque covered bridges, lovely cathedrals and old timbered houses (leaning so precariously, they threaten to tumble into their own shadows). It is a lovely town to explore. The outskirts of Schawbisch Hall are not too pretty - some industrial plants mar the landscape - but the heart of this old town is delightful and offers a nice hotel for the night, the RATSKELLER HOTEL. Although not especially attractive from outside, within, the hotel's public areas offer a wealth of antiques and traditional furnishings. The bedrooms vary from functional modern to country in decor. The Haupt restaurant is staged to create a medieval mood and the Candlelight restaurant is ideal for an intimate evening.

Ratskeller Hotel
Schwabisch Hall

DESTINATION IV　　　HEIDELBERG　　　Hotel Zum Ritter

From Schwabisch Hall head west in the direction of HEILBRONN, an industrial community that is also the largest wine producer in the valley. From Heilbronn continue north along the path of the Neckar river valley. The route travels through fruit orchards languishing in the shadow of sloping vineyards and hillsides dotted with impressive castles. You will drive past BAD FRIEDRICHSHALL, a small town with old salt mines and spas. Your next interesting sightseeing excursion will be to visit the fortress of GUTTENBERG CASTLE, a bird of prey conservation center and one of Europe's largest falconries. Its gamekeeper gives demonstrations with falcons and vultures every day at 11 AM and 3 PM. Perched on the hillside, HORNBERG CASTLE appears as the Neckar follows the bends of the valley. Shortly beyond, the ivy-covered ruins of the 9th-century fortress of EBERBACH can be seen. A final highlight before reaching tonight's destination is the "Gem of the Neckar", the towering HIRSCHHORN CASTLE. Fortified by its keep and sentry wall, this castle has been converted to accommodate overnight guests. Although it is not included in this guide as an overnight stop, you can enjoy lovely views of the Neckar river valley from its open air terrace restaurant.

The Neckar river next rounds a bend to expose the enchanting city of HEIDELBERG. In rich rust tones, Heidelberg's crowning castle, set against a backdrop of contrasting green, creates a spectacular sprawling skyline with its octagonal towers, belfries and gates. A visit to the castle affords a sweeping view of the valley over the pitches and angles of Heidelberg's distinctive old rooftops and buildings.

Heidelberg is a city whose mood is set by its dominating castle, old university and the lovely River Neckar that meanders through its center. This is a city of romance. Goethe fell in love here and the musical career of Schumann, a master of the romantic period, began here. The setting of Heidelberg was the inspiration for "The Student Prince", an opera by Sigmund Romberg that depicts student life as jovial and merry. This wonderful old university town has one main street that is the center of activity and captures most of Heidelberg's atmosphere. The cobbled pedestrian street of Hauptstrasse is bordered on each side with a melange of student taverns, lovely shops and assorted coffee houses. Explore the town: visit the Rathaus, view the stunning cathedral, see the students' punishment cell at the university and walk the few blocks to the picturesque Alte Brucke (Old Bridge).

Then cross the river and enjoy a stroll along Philosophers' Way (Philosophenweg), a path skirting the river - beautiful by day as well as by night when lit by soft lights.

Hotel Zum Ritter
Heidelberg

Hauptstrasse is also the address of the HOTEL ZUM RITTER. Professionally managed by the Kuchemeister family, this hotel affords one of the best locations in town. Its intricate and stately facade is easy to recognize and dates from 1592 when the master builder, Carolus Belier, imprinted the name Zum Ritter in gold. The hotel derives its name from the statue of the young Roman knight which stands atop its gable. Official records show the building served for a decade as a

Rathaus, or town hall, before it became the Hotel Zum Ritter. From its rooftop garden you will have incomparable views of the old city. Although the facade of the Hotel Zum Ritter is wonderful and the dining room decorated in antiques, the bedrooms (with the exception of a few decorated with traditional style furniture) are modern in decor and rather drab. However, the hotel serves a nice breakfast that is included in the price of the room and at night the restaurant is lit with candles and assumes an intimate, romantic mood.

Enjoy the sightseeing and the shopping in the olde worlde city of Heidelberg. Then when it is time to continue your journey, you have many convenient options: you can easily take the expressway south to the Black Forest or north to the Rhine and Moselle, or, if your holidays must end, it is only a short drive to either the Frankfurt or Stuttgart airports.

Heidelberg

The Romantic Road and The Neckar Valley

Bavarian Highlights

MUNICH

Aying

Steingaden

Fussen

Kempten

Pfronten

Austria

Hohenschwangau

Neuschwanstein

Linderhof

Wies

Oberammergau

Ettal

Murnau

Walchensee

Wallgau

STDORF

GARMISCH-
PARTENKIRCHEN

Miltenwald

Bad Wiesee

Gmund

Schliersee

Tegernsee

Bayrischzell

Wall

Neuhaus

Wiessach

Achensee

Reichenall

Walchsee

Reit im Winkl

Labau

Chiemsee

Herrenchiemsee

ISING AM
CHIEMSEE

Salzburg

Bad Reichenall

Kehlstein – Eagle's Nest

BERCHTESGADEN

Ramsau

Hintersee

Konigsee

◉ *Overnight Stops*
★ *Alternate Hotel Choices*
   See Hotel Section of Guide
✈ *Airport*

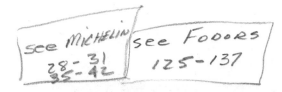

see MICHELIN
28-31
35-42

see FODORS
125-137

81

Bavarian Highlights

It is no wonder that Bavaria is a favorite destination for so many travelers. This small region in the southeastern corner of Germany proudly maintains the reputation of having the friendliest people, the most breathtaking mountains, the quaintest villages, the prettiest lakes and the handsomest castles in Germany.

Neuschwanstein - Mad King Ludwig's Castle

Summertime paints Bavaria's valleys and hillsides with edelweiss, alpine roses and orchids. Winter gently softens the landscape in a carpet of white snow and turns Bavaria into a sportsman's paradise. This is a region where traditional costume is worn with pride. This itinerary traces a route that begins in Munich, Germany's "secret capital city", dips briefly into Austria to visit Salzburg, winds through Bavarian hamlets, visits the resort towns of Garmisch-Partenkirchen and Oberammergau, highlights Ludwig II's fairytale castles and concludes in the splendid Allgau region.

ORIGINATING CITY   MUNICH

Bavaria is an enchanting region and Munich, the "gateway to Bavaria", stars as one of Europe's most beautiful cities. Munich, a wonderful crusty old beer-drinking, music-loving city, rivals Paris and London with its excellent shopping and traditional architecture. The heart of the city is magical to explore on foot, and a logical place to start is at the main train station. From there, go directly towards the Stachus. This square is officially called the Karlsplatz, after Elector Karl Theodor, but the townspeople had such a high regard for Foderl Stachus, that they named the square after him in 1730. Leaving the Stachus, wander under Karlstor Gate into the pedestrian zone of the old city that is laced with fountains, fruit stands, ballad singers and lay preachers. Off to the left notice the Renaissance facade of St Michael's and behind it the Cathedral, "Frauenkirche", both a landmark and symbol of the city. Marienplatz is just a short distance farther. This is a dramatically beautiful square and serves as the heart of the shopping district and the historical core of the city. The clock on the town hall strikes 11 AM and little figures emerge from around the clock to perform a jousting tournament. Awaiting the hour is a perfect excuse to sit at one of the little cafes in the square for some refreshment before continuing on with your sightseeing.

Since the main business district of Munich has been converted to a pedestrian mall, window shopping is a pleasure. Peek into some of the beautiful shops then take a short walk over to Munich's oldest parish church, Alter Peter, with its impressive 11th-century interior. Climb its tower for a panoramic view which on a clear day extends to the Alps. Just a short walk from the Alter Peter church is the Viktualienmarkt, a permanent market that flavors the city with glimpses of the past. Meander through the Burgasse to Alter Hof, the first Residence of the city. Then straight on to Maxi-Joseph-Platz where you will discover the National Theater and Residence, and catch a glimpse of the Maximilianeum at the end of Maxmilianstrasse. Continue along the Residenzstrasse with a glance into the lovely inner courtyards of the Residence and on to Odeonsplatz, then circle back to the station via Brienner Strasse, Maximiliansplatz and the Stachus.

Although removed from the heart of the city, a few other sights deserve mention. The Deutsche Museum (the German Museum), is often referred to as "Germany's Smithsonian" and is known for its diverse collection of scientific and technological displays. The BMW Museum is interesting to car buffs as well as to those who understand the importance of the business to the financial welfare and history of Munich. The Alte Pinakothek, a museum, has an incredible display of works by 14th-to 18th-century masters such as Raphael, Michelangelo, Van Dyck, Rembrandt, Breughel, Goya and Titian. The Neue Pinakothek, whose collection is limited to 19th-century artists, is a relatively new structure replacing the original 19th-century building that was destroyed in the Second World War. The Haus der Kunst, located on the edge of the English Garden, has a continually changing art collection. If time and weather permit, walk the length of the gardens to the student district of Schwabing. On Munich's outskirts is Schloss Nymphenburg, the summer palace. Built in 1664 with additions in the 18th century, it is a beautiful architectural example of baroque and rococo styles. One might also want to detour out to the Olympic Park, site of the 1972 Games.

Fall of course translates as the "Oktoberfest" and many from all over the world congregate in Munich to participate in the festivities. This happy, noisy celebration of the sausage and the hops begins in September and concludes on the first Sunday in October. The festival confines itself to a meadow in southwestern Munich called the Theresienwiese.

Whatever the season, enjoy Munich for its opera, theater, shopping, beauty, character and history. A central and wonderful place to stay is the PREYSING HOTEL. It is just a fifteen to twenty-minute walk from the hotel's front door to the heart of the city's shopping and sightseeing. Service at the Preysing Hotel is gracious and very personalized. The bedrooms are furnished with extremely comfortable beds, down comforters covered in pressed white linen, a desk and a few prints. The decor is attractive in its simplicity. The hotel has an excellent restaurant, open for both lunch and dinner. A lavish breakfast is served in the downstairs restaurant or on a trolley in the privacy of your room.

DESTINATION I   ISING AM CHIEMSEE   Zum Goldenen Pflug

Leave Munich by traveling the autoroute southwest in the direction of Salzburg for an approximate two-hour drive to CHIEMSEE to discover the HOTEL ZUM GOLDENEN PFLUG and enjoy its glorious setting near the shores of the lake. Often a hotel focuses its energies on and shows a preference for either its accommodations or its restaurant. However, under the special management of Hartwig Leyk, pride and care are evident in every aspect of the Hotel Zum Goldenen Pflug. The reception area and spacious inviting bar are found surprisingly in what were once the cow byres. The charming dining rooms, Fischer Stube, Gaststube and Jagerstube are found in the barn. All three restaurants benefit from the same delightful presentation of menu and courses but vary a little in atmosphere. The bedrooms are scattered around the complex and, depending on their location, vary in theme of decor but all contain exceptional furniture.   Zum Goldenen Pflug, translated as the golden plow, is a gem of an inn conveniently located in the little farming village of Ising, just a short distance from the shores of the serene Chiemsee.

Zum Goldenen Pflug
Ising am Chiemsee

Against a backdrop of magnificent peaks, Chiemsee is the largest lake in the foothills of Bavaria.   Although not as beautiful as some of Germany's other lakes which are tucked into mountain pockets, the lake is a draw for sport enthusiasts and has two islands of interest to travelers: FRAUENCHIEMSEE and HERREN-CHIEMSEE.   As early as the 8th century, Frauenchiemsee was a home for Benedictine nuns.   In 866 Irmengard, a great-granddaughter of Charlemagne, was buried here.   Herrenchiemsee is an island chosen by King Ludwig II for the setting of his Bavarian Versailles - Neues Schloss.   Although construction ceased at the time of the king's death in 1866, with only the center of the enormous palace completed, it includes a stunning replica of Versailles' Great Hall of Mirrors with sumptuous and elaborate detailing.   The surrounding gardens and forest are most definitely worth a visit. You take a boat to this small island and at the pier are horse-drawn carriages to whisk you to the castle. Of course you can also walk, but should it be a rainy day, the carriages are a welcome sight.

DESTINATION II   BERCHTESGADEN   Hotel Geiger

Leaving the Chiemsee, continue east along the scenic autoroute following the signs for Salzburg. As you near the Austrian border, the Alps are visible in the distance and onion-capped spires crown the rolling hills in the foreground. This is a rich farming area with cattle, sheep, weathered barns and Tyrolean homes dressing the green landscape.

Although in Austria, SALZBURG is just on the border and much too close to pass without visiting. This delightful city, located on both banks of the Salzach river, is dramatically set at the base of the Kapuzinerberg and Monchsberg mountains. The ruins of its fortress straddle the city skyline. In the old section of town, narrow streets wind amongst the city's many fine baroque buildings which shelter a number of exquisite shops and boutiques. Salzburg is the birthplace of Wolfgang Amadeus Mozart and when the Mozart Festival is held annually here in the months of July and August, the town is bursting with song and gaiety (and tourists). Regardless of the season Salzburg is an enchanting city. This itinerary just touches on the glories of Salzburg, one of Austria's many fascinating destinations. If you have the luxury of more time and would like to extend your holiday to include more of Austria, another guide in the Travel Press series, AUSTRIAN COUNTRY INNS & CASTLES, can provide you with a wealth of information.

Leave Salzburg and cross the border back into Germany and then travel just a few miles south into the Alps to the mountain village of BERCHTESGADEN. Found at one end of the German Alpine Road, Berchtesgaden, an ancient market town, is now a very popular winter sports resort. Explore the Schlossplatz (the picturesque castle square) and follow the meandering 16th-century arcade to the market place. Berchtesgaden's noblest old inns and interesting houses are located here and many bear the details of weathered woodcarvings that the Augustinian monks introduced to the region in the Middle Ages. Also popular to explore are the Salt Mines of Berchtesgaden, located only a few miles away near the Austrian border. Salt was a principal source of the town's prosperity in the early 16th century. The tour is dramatic and includes a trip down a 500-meter chute, an endless web of tunnels and a journey by raft across an illuminated subterranean lake.

On the north edge of town is a marvelous chalet, the HOTEL GEIGER. With its weathered exterior, attractively decked with green shutters, wooden balconies and overflowing flower boxes, the Hotel Geiger blends perfectly into this Alpine region. The entrance into the main building exposes the beauty of a wood paneled dining room, handsome wood painted ceilings, planked floors, heart carved chairs, red print cushions, Oriental carpets, hand carved figurines on the chandeliers, pewter, candles, antlers and the soft ticking of old clocks, an atmosphere reminiscent of a fine Scottish hunting lodge. As a final bonus, large windows open to spectacular Alpine views. There are forty bedrooms in the main building and ten in a new annex: all enjoy views of the mountains.

With the Hotel Geiger as your base, you can enjoy the town and its shopping, take advantage of trails that leave practically from the Geiger's doorstep and visit the dazzling lake of Konigsee and the dramatic Eagle's Nest.

Located 3 miles south of Berchtesgaden, KONIGSEE'S setting and beauty is comparable to some of the world's most magnificent fjords. Steep Alpine walls enclose this romantic lake that is accessible from the tip of its one small resort village. Traffic on the lake is restricted to electric boats in an admirable effort to minimize pollution. The boats provide the only access and method to fully explore the lake. They glide from the docks across a glass-like, brilliant green lake and wind round the bend to view the picturesque 18th-century chapel and settlement at St Bartholomae where the postcard-pretty little church is built on a pocket of land near the edge of the lake. A backdrop of maple trees and mountains completes the idyllic scene.

The dramatic peak of KEHLSTEIN and the serene pastoral plateau of the Obersalzberg are located just east of Berchtesgaden along a winding Alpine road. The last stretch of just a few miles on the approach to the Kehlstein, the highest road in Germany, must be traveled by postal bus. At its crest is a foreboding granite walled structure that was built by Adolf Hitler and understandably labeled the EAGLE'S NEST. To reach Hitler's retreat, an elevator negotiates the last 400 feet through a shaft in the Kehlstein mountain.

Hotel Geiger
Berchtesgaden

Hopefully you will have a sunny day to coincide with your departure from Berchtesgaden.   Keep your passport at hand as today you will be criss-crossing back and forth between Germany and Austria.   The Alps are incredible against blue skies or dramatic as they break through lingering clouds.   Take the Alpine Road (Alpinstrasse) in the direction of Ramsau.   Spring weather exposes green foothills and glimpses of jagged peaks struggling with the quickly disappearing fog. The road follows a stream that cuts along and through rocky foothills.   Chalets sit perched on knolls as green as a golf course fairway.   RAMSAU'S church has a picture-perfect setting, silhouetted against the Alpine peaks.   Take a detour of 6 kilometers at Ramsau to HINTERSEE, which, on a still morning, is a gorgeous lake reflecting the chalet homes and overpowering mountains of Reiter Alps.

An old cobblestoned road winds up from Ramsau in the direction of TRAUNSTEIN, enhanced by breathtaking views of surrounding peaks.   For the photographer, old weathered chalets are tucked on knolls with firewood stacked exactly at their side and milk pails set full and lined up for collection.   The German Alpine Road reaches a crest and then descends into a farther valley.   The village of SAALACHTERJELTNBERG sits in a shaded valley not far from Saalachsee. Cross the Saalach river and continue in the direction of Traunstein.   Soon after a road branches off to BAD REICHENALL, look back for a dramatic view of the Gletschhorn framed by the valley walls.   Before the village of RAUSCHBERG turn off towards RUHPOLDING, following the Alpine Road signs.   There are no major towns along this stretch between Rauschberg and Reit im Winkl - only lakes, hiking trails, breathtaking vistas and an occasional farmer, dressed in Tyrolean green, sitting on a tractor.   The road starts to climb again, then levels out following the valley.   With every turn of the road, mountains present themselves from a different intriguing perspective.   From the small hamlet of LABAU, the road twists and winds with the narrow valley and at Seehause you enter the region of lovely small lakes including Lodensee, Mittersee and Weitsee - all especially pretty when the sun shines and the lakes mirror the surrounding scenery.

Ramsau

REIT IM WINKL is a quaint hamlet - a cluster of chalets. The road continues in the direction of Kossen and the Austrian border, with the peaks in the distance ever-beckoning. The road narrows after crossing the border as it follows the path of the Tyrolean Alps.

From KOSSEN follow signs to WALCHSEE. Just 7 kilometers away, Walchsee is a small lake with a beautiful setting: the Pyramidenspitze seems to rise right out of the opposite shore. Pass through the town of DURCHHOLZEN NIEDERNDORF before crossing back over the Inn River into Germany. OBEANDORF is a busy but little village. Continue now in the direction of NIEDERNDORF and then watch for signs to Bayrischzell. Turn onto what seems a small country road and wind through the valley 20 kilometers to Bayrischzell. En route is the hillside village of WALL with spectacular rolling valley vistas and striking snow covered peaks. REICHENAU is a hamlet of only two or three chalets. Here the road is dotted with strategically placed benches on which people settle to knit, read the morning paper, or just to soak in the view and let the day pass at will. The road is glorious as it winds through the mountains.

BAYRISCHZELL is a picture-book ski village, a perfect spot to picnic. Buy bread at the local bakery, and picnic on the square by the church. Leave Bayrischzell following signs to Schliersee and Miesbach. NEUHAUS is a town at the tip of Schliersee with a striking 17th-century church set just past the train track. From Neuhaus the road follows the contours of the lake and winds around to its other side where the village of SCHLIERSEE is nestled on its shore. This is a pretty village whose two church spires reflect in the lake - a postcard-perfect setting.

HAUSHAM is just 1 kilometer away, newer, with industry on its outskirts. From Hausham follow signs to Tegernsee. At GMUND skirt the Tegernsee on its northern shores to SAPPLFELD just a few kilometers before the town of BAD WIESSEE. This is a town of green lawns that roll lazily down to the water's edge - a scene enhanced by mighty mountain peaks towering just a shadow away. If you did not picnic in Bayrischzell and are now hungry or ready to slow the pace, you could end your day's journey here at the LANDHAUS SAPPLFELD. The hotel is a bit difficult to find, set amongst residential houses, but watch for the Hotel Weissenhof on the outskirts of Bad Wiessee and turn left. At this point you will see signs posted to direct you the short distance farther on to the Landhaus Sapplfeld.

If you opt to continue, at the town of WEISSACH turn towards Achensee. The road winds in a valley along the Weissach river and touches the Austrian border at Achenpass. The road soon travels around a dam whose water is a beautiful aquamarine color and the Zwiesler and Demehoch peaks tower above. Scenery now changes to a more wooded landscape; the rolling green pastures simply seem to disappear. At LENGGRIES VORDEREISS pay the nominal toll of 4 DM and take a private road, a beautiful but slow drive, through pine trees and across rugged terrain. Hohergrauwig and Soiernspitze are broad chiseled peaks at the mouth of the valley. This is a lovely approach into the town of WALLGAU.

With an absolutely magnificent setting for a village - ringed by the peaks of the Karwendel mountains - MITTENWALD is a holiday resort that is known worldwide. In addition to its beauty, this village is famous for the crafting of fine violins, and the Geigenbau (violin) Museum is interesting to visit. Soon after Mittenwald, the rolling green hills return dotted with weathered sheds. It is a gentle half hour's drive on to the Alpine resort village of Garmisch-Partenkirchen.

Framed by some of Germany's most dramatic, jagged peaks, GARMISCH-PART-ENKIRCHEN is backed up against her highest - the towering Zugspitze. At one time two villages, Garmisch and Partenkirchen merged to meet the demands of accommodating the 1936 winter Olympic Games. The distinction between what were once two towns is still apparent. Garmisch is a bustle of activity, with broader, newer streets lined by larger stores and hotels, and closer to the slopes. Partenkirchen, with narrow winding streets and timbered buildings, preserves more olde worlde charm. The POSTHOTEL PARTENKIRCHEN is a marvelous hotel that reflects the character of its past as a posting station and the tradition of service and standard that four generations of the Stahl family have strived to achieve. The bedrooms are attractively decorated with cherished antiques, lovely prints and nice fabrics. A few rooms enjoy unobstructed views of the Zugspitze. For additional information on this region, please see page 29 of the GERMANY BY RAIL, BOAT AND BUS itinerary.

Posthotel Partenkirchen
Garmisch-Partenkirchen

Garmisch-Partenkirchen is an ideal base from which to explore the charming Alpine region of the Oberallgau. With Garmisch bracketing one end and the Bodensee on the western boundary, this area of the Bavarian Highlands includes not only such popular destinations as Ludwig's Neuschwanstein, but also some little known mountain villages that are tucked away in a Bavaria of yesteryear. This is a land of flowering meadows and snow capped peaks. The Oberallgau is glorious when blue skies warm endless hiking trails and charming river valleys, and in winter it is a lively sports center. Bavaria's young King Ludwig II's family home, Hohenschwangau, is located here and he chose the region for its splendor and spectacular setting to build his dream castles, Neuschwanstein and Linderhof.

This itinerary will outline a circular route to visit the castles and highlights of the region: they are all within an easy drive of Garmisch-Partenkirchen and the trip could easily be scheduled over a few days.

North of Garmisch-Partenkirchen, on the road to Oberammergau, is the small town of ETTAL. Ettal is famous for its baroque monastery, pilgrimage church and the herbal liqueur that is produced by the resident monks. It is near Ettal where you will need to watch for a small sign directing you to the isolated castle of Linderhof.

King Ludwig II intended to rule his kingdom from five castles. Ludwig began his reign at the young age of eighteen, but he soon tired of politics and began building castles. Only three were partially completed before his mysterious death at age forty in 1886. LINDERHOF is the smallest of his accomplishments. Set in the loneliness of the Ammer mountains, this elegant palace is rich in its furnishings and spectacular with its landscaped gardens. It is a lovely shaded walk from where you buy a ticket to the castle. Be sure to buy an English translation of the tour at the entrance, as there aren't always enough English speaking guests to warrant a special guide. Both the interior and gardens are well worth a visit. Ludwig's bedroom looks out onto a dramatic cascading fountain bordered by a wisteria-covered arbor that is beautiful in bloom. A highlight of the grounds includes a man-made grotto on the hillside above the castle that Ludwig commissioned for a dramatic staging of the operas of Richard Wagner.

Continue on from Linderhof in the direction of the Austrian border. Border controls are very lax, however a passport is required to cross back and forth between Germany and Austria. This routing affords a tempting glimpse of the peaceful Austrian countryside and avoids backtracking in order to visit Neuschwanstein and Hohenschwangau. The drive through Austria takes you along the shores of a serene lake and onto the village of REUTTE, tucked into a valley pocket and shadowed by the towering peaks of the Ammer Range. MUSAU is another typically charming Austrian village you'll pass before crossing back into Germany and on to the colorful spa town of FUSSEN. Note: "Konigschlossen" translates as King's Castles. Coming back into Germany directions to the castles are given in German.

HOHENSCHWANGAU was built by the Knights of the Swan. It burned in 1600 and was rebuilt from ruins by Maximilian II of Bavaria between 1832 and 1836. He was the father of Ludwig II, and Hohenschwangau became their family residence. There are a few designated parking areas below the castle and it requires a steep climb on foot from any of the parking lots to tour Hohenschwangau. The history of Ludwig's life is outlined on the tour and the rooms that reflect the family's style of living are interesting to visit. It was at Hohenschwangau that Ludwig first met his beloved Wagner.

NEUSCHWANSTEIN towers above Hohenschwangau. From the bedroom of his family home Ludwig could watch the construction of his fairytale fortress. A visit to both castles requires three to four hours depending on crowds and the season. If time dictates choosing between the two, Neuschwanstein is a must.

To reach Neuschwanstein, you can tackle the half hour walk up a steep path, ride the shuttle bus, or take advantage of the slower but more romantic horse-drawn carriage. Regardless of method of approach, the very last stretch to this fanciful castle must be on foot. Perched on a rocky ledge, high above the valley, Neuschwanstein was Walt Disney's inspiration for Sleeping Beauty's castle. Designed by a theater set designer and an eccentric king, the interior is a romantic flight of fancy whose rooms afford spectacular views. Ludwig lived in a dream world set to music by his adored friend, Richard Wagner, whose work and scenes from his operas are found throughout in the decor.

Leave Hohenschwangau and Neuschwanstein, travel north in the direction of STEINGADEN and from there continue east following signs to Oberammergau. Soon after crossing the dramatic bridge outside Steingaden, take a short detour to visit WIES and its lovely church. This ornately baroque church is spectacular for the setting it creates - a lovely white facade, capped with an impressive onion dome, set against the rolling Bavarian landscape.

The road winds back in the direction of Garmisch-Partenkirchen through the picturesque village of OBERAMMERGAU. Oberammergau is a lovely Alpine resort with stunning murals painted on many of its homes and buildings. Every ten years the "Passion Spiel" (Passion Play), a religious play, is performed here. All the residents in town are involved in the production and performance of this play which celebrates the end of the misery and death associated with the Black Plague. The last decade performance was in 1980, but a special 1984 production was held to celebrate the 350-year anniversary of the very first play. The next Passion Play will be held in 1990. In between plays it seems that everyone in the village carves so the shops are filled with lovely wood carvings, a specialty being nativity scenes.

From Oberammergau it is a short drive to Garmisch-Partenkirchen.

DESTINATION IV	OBERSTDORF	Haus Wiese

Depending on what sightseeing you want to include in the vicinity of Garmisch-Partenkirchen, choose your own routing to FUSSEN and then plan on the luxury of a leisurely drive through the charming villages that are tucked away in the scenic Oberallgau. The route exposes one delightful village after another nestled up against the base of the mountains. Venture off on roads that detour through the small ski hamlets. The ski terrain appears gentle and not very challenging, but the ambiance of the region is reflected in each town.

KEMPTEN is the capital of the Allgau region. A cheese-making town, Kempten is the home of Allgauer cheese, similar to Gruyere, and at many cheese dairies villagers can be observed churning cheese by hand. The city's main square, the Kornhausplatz, is romantic and dominated by the Allgau Folklore Museum. This building dates from 1666 and is one of the finest examples of baroque architecture.

From Kempten follows signs south to OBERSTDORF, a village that will prove an ideal base and perfect setting for the conclusion of this Bavarian Highlights itinerary. Oberstdorf is the principal resort in the area and is huddled in a valley against Alpine peaks. The surrounding mountains provide a multitude of ski areas to choose from. The village is a charming mix of narrow streets, lovely stores, taverns and inviting restaurants. It wears the spirit of a resort town and reflects the gaiety of its visitors.

Haus Wiese
Oberstdorf

Otto and Christa Wiese left their home in Hamburg to live in what they consider the most beautiful region in Germany, the Oberallgau. They have settled in Oberstdorf and have opened their home and inn to guests from all over the world. Located on the edge of town, the windows of the HAUS WIESE open up to either green fields or an expanse of white snow and across to the town set against the mountains that enclose it.

From Oberstdorf it is a comfortable drive back to Munich or a convenient drive on to the Bodensee and Konstanz where you can connect with the BLACK FOREST itinerary.

Schleswig Holstein - the Land Between the Seas

Kampen
KIETUM
Westerland
Denmark
Hornum
Niebull
Glucksburg Castle
Flensburg
Amrun
Halligen
Baltic Sea
North Sea
Holm
Schleswig
ALT DUVENSTEDT
Bistensee
Holzbunge Kiel
Molfsee
Freilichtmuseum
Malente-Gremsmuhlen
Sielbeck
Plon
Kellersee
Grosser Plonersee
Eutin
Scharbeutz-Haffkrug
Timmendorfer Strand
Travemunde
Lubeck

◉ Overnight Stops
★ Alternate Hotel Choices
  See Hotel Section of Guide
✈ Airport   🚂 Train — Car

◉ HAMBURG

99

Schleswig Holstein - the Land Between the Seas

Schleswig Holstein is Germany's most northerly province. With Denmark at its tip, this broad finger of land divides the placid Baltic from the wild North Sea. Along the North Sea shore, dykes protect the sky-wide landscape from being claimed by the sea's crashing waves. Safe behind dykes, sheep and cattle graze while crops grow in serene pastures. Offshore, dune-fringed islands brave the sea. Any visit to Schleswig Holstein would not be complete without a trip to one of the islands, so this itinerary takes you and your car atop a train for a rocking ride across the Hindenburgdamm to Sylt. This island boasts an impressive landscape of sand dunes and exposed steep cliffs sheltering quaint little thatched villages from bracing sea breezes. In sharp contrast, the Baltic seacoast is hilly with long graceful fjords extending far inland from the gentle lapping ocean. Here miles and miles of white sand beaches provide a holiday haven for northern Europeans who brave the chilly waters and relax in gaily colored canopied beach chairs while their children decorate sand castles with sea shells. Between these two seas lies Holsteinische Schweiz, "Swiss District", a confusing name as there are no mountain peaks, just a lovely area of wooded rolling hills sprinkled with sparkling lakes.

Northern weather tends to be cool and rainy so pack your warm sweaters and rain gear. But be prepared to be surprised - the weather is unpredictable so hopefully you will have balmy cloudless days as you explore this lovely region far from the beaten tourist paths.

ORIGINATING CITY   HAMBURG

Hamburg is a mighty trading and industrial center on the banks of the River Elbe. Understandably, Hamburg was a target for Second World War bombings - by the end of the war the town was little more than a heap of rubble. But with great determination, much of the city has been rebuilt in the old style so that today it has the mellow feel of an older age.

Hamburg's sights are spread around a large area, so the most efficient way to get from place to place is on the U-Bahn, or subway system, whose stations are marked on the city's tourist map. Include the following on your sightseeing agenda: St Michael's church (Hamburg's symbol), the palatial city hall built at the end of the 19th century, the art museum, an hour-long tour of the harbor to see the boats from the world's great trading nations, a peaceful three-hour tour of the Alster Lake and canals that run through the heart of the city, and shopping along the Spitalerstrasse and Monckebergstrasse.

Just a short walk for sailors from their ships, Hamburg's notorious red-light district has grown up along the Reeperbahn and surrounding streets, where erotic entertainment knows no bounds. This raunchy area, just west of the city center, is just a ripple in what is otherwise a very straight-laced city.

If you are in Hamburg on a Sunday morning, plan on visiting the Altona Fish Market, an open air market at the water's edge, offering everything - fruit, flowers, rabbits, socks, antiques and, of course, fish. The show starts at six, but plan on arriving by nine. No need to eat before you arrive; there are plenty of food stands selling everything from delicious hot grilled sausages to crunchy rolls filled with smoked eel or pickled herring.

The HOTEL PREM is suggested as your hotel in Hamburg if you are staying over prior to starting this itinerary. Set in an elegant townhouse with the Alster Lake at its front and a tranquil garden at its rear, the hotel commands a handsome location. The downstairs is small - a lounge area leading to a bar and beyond an airy restaurant overlooking the garden. The bedrooms, accented with lovely antiques, have high ceilings giving a spacious feeling. A few lovely rooms have the original ornate plasterwork ceilings. The staff could not be kinder. The joys of this small hotel more than compensate for its location which, although beautiful, is just a little too far to walk to the center of town.

DESTINATION I   ALT DUVENSTEDT   Hotel Topferhaus

After a few days of city adventures, you will be ready for a change - something quiet and relaxed, a complete change of pace from the bustling city.

The traffic in and around Hamburg is difficult - a surging mass of cars traveling at breakneck speed. Drive into the downtown area and follow signs for the autobahn 1 to LUBECK. About an hour's drive finds you outside Lubeck's impressive Holstenor Gate, a squat fortress crowned by twin towers shaped like enormous witches' hats. The gate guards the entrance to the medieval old town set on an island surrounded by canals and waterways. This sheltered port was the leading city of the Hanseatic League, a group of towns who banded together for trade advantages during the 13th to 16th centuries. Park your car and head for the marketplace in the old town, where the Rathaus, Lubeck's impressive town hall, covers two sides of the square. Nearby, the tall, slender twin steeples of the Marienkirche, St Mary's church, rise above the town. Step inside to admire the lofty fan ceiling of this majestic building.

Leaving the old town of Lubeck, drive to the north for fifteen minutes to the popular Baltic resort of TRAVEMUNDE. It is fun to drive along its riverfront road seeing the boats and ferries on one side and the crowded little seaside shops on the other and then to drive along its wide sandy beach fringed by modern hotels.

As you leave Travemunde, follow the road 76 that parallels the coastline going north. If the weather is sunny and warm, you may want to get into the German holiday spirit and join the crowds on the beaches at the coastal resorts of TIMMENDORFER STRAND or SCHARBEUTZ-HAFFKRUG. In pleasant weather sun worshipers soak up the sun from the shelter of their canopied beach chairs while offshore the Baltic waters come alive with the sails of gaily colored sailing boats and wind surfers.

Follow highway 76 as it turns inland at Scharbeutz-Haffkrug. Leaving the flat coastal landscape behind you, enter a region of gently undulating farmland sprinkled with lakes both large and small. Narrow threads of land often separate one lake from another. The region is known as "Holsteinische Schweiz", the "Swiss district", not because of its Alpine peaks, of which there are none, but because it shares a similar rock formation with Switzerland. About a half hour's drive brings you to the lakeside town of EUTIN. Drive through the town, park by the old moated castle and stroll through the adjacent lakefront park to capture views of the EUTINER SEE.

Farther lovely lake vistas are provided by the drive around the KELLER SEE to MALENTE-GREMSMUHLEN. Take the road along the northern shore through SIELBECK for the prettiest views. The town of Gremsmuhlen is the departure point for motor-boat tours of the beautiful five lakes to the west of town. The frustration of catching only glimpses of the lakes through the trees is removed when you glide along them on a boat.

Just a short distance to the west is PLON, the most picturesque town in the area. The town sits atop a small hill overlooking the region's largest lake, the GROSSER PLONNERSEE. Drive through the town to the quaint cobbled marketplace near the church. Park your car and walk up the narrow cobblestoned alley to the castle terrace where you have a lovely view of the lake below.

Hotel Topferhaus
Alt Duvenstedt

Leaving Plon, you follow the road 76 for the half hour's drive to the outskirts of KIEL. Unless you are interested in busy freight and yacht harbors, do not go into the city but take the road 404 to the B4 and on to the suburban town of MOLFSEE. Here you will find the FREILICHTMUSEUM, Schleswig-Holstein's Open Air Museum, a collection of rustic farms and country homes dating from the 16th through the 19th centuries that have been brought here and reassembled. It is great fun to watch the local craftsmen operating the old smithy, potter's shop, mill and bakehouse. You can explore the old houses and barns and retire to the timbered inn for welcome refreshments. Note: the park is closed between November and April and on Mondays except in July and August.

It is only about a half hour's drive from the museum to your hotel. Take the autobahn 215 south towards Hamburg for just a few miles. The autobahn 215 merges with the autobahn 7 and you turn north on the 7 following signs for Flensburg and the Danish border. Your exit is marked RENDSBURG. As you leave the autobahn, turn right away from Rendsburg: a few minutes bring you to the tiny village of HOLZBUNGE. Turn left through the village and you will find the HOTEL TOPFERHAUS on the southern shore of the BISTENSEE just a short drive from the village.

Isolated and lovely, the whitewashed thatched hotel overlooks the lake. The inside is loaded with superb antiques. The owners have a real eye for beautiful beds, armoirs and chests. Most of the bedrooms have views of the peaceful lake gently lapping in front of the hotel. An adjacent farmhouse-style building houses the elegant rustic RESTAURANT TOPFERHAUS.

DESTINATION II   KEITUM-SYLT   Benen Diken Hof

When it is time to leave the peaceful waters of the Bistensee, take the road north to the ancient Viking stronghold of SCHLESWIG. The old town (Altstadt) hugs the northern bank of the Schlei inlet: its cathedral dates from the 12th century and is noted for its handsome carved altar. Further along the inlet you come to the picturesque fishermen's district of HOLM. Stroll down some of its quaint lanes that lead to the fishing boats at the water's edge.

Museum lovers will want to drive to the SCHLOSS GOTTORF located on a small island at the west end of the town. The castle contains two museums: the state's museum of art, handicraft and folklore collection and the prehistorical museum. Even if you are not a museum devotee, you will be impressed by the very old Viking ship, the Nydam Boot. Long and slender, the Nydam Boot conjures up pictures of fast ships and a race of fierce, proud seamen who reached the limits of the known world in their elegant sleek craft.

A short autobahn drive connects Schleswig with FLENSBURG, but if the weather is fine, take advantage of the pretty coastal route that parallels the Schlei inlet and the Baltic coast. Near the tip of the Flensburg fjord GLUCKSBURG CASTLE comes into view, apparently floating on the lake that once provided its defenses.

The road traces the fjord through MURWIK to the maritime port of Flensburg. Follow the signs directing you west across the marshes to NIEBUL. Do not go into the town, but follow the well-posted signs of a car atop a railway car for the train to SYLT. You cannot drive your car to the island, but take it on top of a railway carriage along the causeway that connects the island to the mainland. There is no need to make advance reservations - you purchase your ticket as you drive into the railway yard. Do not worry about catching a particular train for there are between eleven and sixteen departures each day.

Leaving the ticket office, you drive your car onto the train and sit in it for the 50-minute bumping ride past fields of sheep and Holstein cows towards the shoals that lead to the Hindenburg Levee that connects the island to the mainland. From your lofty perch atop the train you can appreciate the centuries-long battle to keep the sea from flooding this flat low-lying land. A series of dykes protects the land from the water and the farms are built on earthen banks that become islands if the dykes fail. Crossing the sea dyke, the train arrives in the island capital, WESTERLAND, a town of elegant boutiques and sophisticated nightspots.

There are many small hotels on Sylt but, if you want to splurge, choose the island's loveliest hotel, the BENEN DIKEN HOF in KEITUM. Set in the island's most picturesque village, the hotel is several squat thatched Friesian farmhouses joined into a complex by means of glass corridors that appear to bring the outdoors inside. Decorated throughout in white and cream with accents of pale pink and blue, the hotel is "decorator perfect" - warm and welcoming. After a walk along the sand dunes in the bracing sea air, you can return to the hotel to pamper yourself with a sauna and a massage or a relaxing swim.

*Benen Diken Hof
Keitum-Sylt*

The hotel's greatest asset is Claas Johannsen, the owner and manager. An avid volunteer fireman, his fondest memory of his one trip to the United States is the morning he spent riding around New York's streets with the fire department. Of an evening he can be found operating the hotel's cozy bar surrounded by his collection of old model fire engines. His warmth and graciousness transcend the language barrier.

The lovely restaurant at the Benen Diken Hof serves only breakfast, but do not worry: the small island abounds with restaurants. A particular recommendation goes to the RESTAURANT LANDHAUS STRICKER in the adjacent village of TINNUM - gourmet dining in elegant surroundings in an adorable old Friesian farmhouse.

Keitum occupies a sheltered site and remains an old Friesian village of squat thatched cottages, lilac bushes and tree-lined streets. Keitum's low-slung houses are topped by thick roofs of reeds gathered from the tidal marshes, just the kind of house from which you would expect Hansel and Gretel to emerge. High garden walls protect against storm flood tides and winds. The lovely old village has two splendid museums: the Old Friesian House and the Sylter Country Museum. Built in 1739 by a sailing captain, the red brick old Friesian farmhouse passed into the hands of a 19th-century historian who assembled a history of the island. The house and the furnishings are such that a Friesian of two centuries ago would feel immediately at home. Nearby on Cliff Street you find the Country Museum, another old sea captain's home that contains collections of island seafaring memorabilia and coins, porcelain and costumes dating back hundreds of years. Inspired perhaps by their forefathers, modern artisans have set up their shops in nearby houses.

As you explore farther afield, you pass Keitum's St Severin church, a landmark for seafarers since it was built seven centuries ago. The island's days as an important maritime center are long past, yet once a year, on the eve of February 22nd, the islanders pile straw, reeds and wood into a huge bonfire as a symbolic send-off for the island's sailors.

The island is lovely, a long narrow strip, much of it sand dunes facing the North Sea. Dykes, sand dunes and cliffs protect the island from North Sea storms. Twenty-five miles of white sand attract summer sun worshipers - bathing suits are as welcome as none - and canopied beach chairs provide snug shelter from the wind. Hardy Germans enjoy swimming in the chill North Sea waves, but you will probably find the hotel's heated swimming pool, complete with wave making machine, more to your liking.

Devote a day to exploring the island and its villages huddled behind the sand dunes, then use the remainder of your stay for relaxation - walking or exploring other islands. Ferries depart from the bustling harbor at HORNUM for the nearby island of AMRUM or for a sightseeing tour of the "mini islands" known as HALLIGEN. On these little islands, man has battled the sea for centuries. The farmhouses are built on man-made hills because the sea regularly floods the pastures leaving the farmhouses marooned on their own miniature islands.

When your island holiday is over, if your destination is Denmark, you can take a ferry from List or retrace your steps to Niebul for the short drive to the Danish border. For those who are returning to Hamburg, follow the road south across the flat polder lands which have been reclaimed from the sea. The waters offshore are shallow; sea dykes keep them at bay, protecting the lush green pasture and farmlands behind.

The Train to Sylt

Schleswig Holstein - the Land Between the Seas

Fairytale Country and The Harz Mountains

GOSLAR

Schulenberg

Clausthal-Zellerfeld

Torfhaus

Altenau

BRAUNLAGE

St. Andreasburg

Uslar

Herzberg

SABABURG

Gottingen

Hann Munden

Kassel

Bauntal

Spangenberg

Rotenberg an der Fulda

Bebra

BAD HERSFELD

Alsfeld

FRANKFURT

⊚ Overnight Stops
★ Alternate Hotel Choices
See Hotel Section of Guide

111

Fairytale Country and the Harz Mountains

No less entrancing than Germany's more oft' trod tourist routes is the region between Frankfurt and Hanover - the region that gave birth to "Sleeping Beauty" and "Little Red Riding Hood", whose tales beginning "Once upon a time" transport us back to childhood memories of wicked stepmothers and handsome princes. But the area has more than fairytales: it is enhanced by its misty mountains, neat small towns of half-timbered buildings and placid shallow rivers flowing quietly through pretty countryside. It was here that Jacob and Wilhelm Grimm pursued their hobby of writing down folktales told to them by the local villagers. A published collection of these tales is known worldwide as "Grimm's Fairy Tales".

Hann Munden

This itinerary highlights the heart of the German fairytale route and then swings east into the Harz mountains. The itinerary does not correspond exactly with the German Tourist Office fairytale route, yet it is similar and the German Tourist Office will be glad to provide you with a whimsical pictorial map to lead you down the Fairytale Road which is well marked by signposts with a smiling good fairy.

ORIGINATING CITY   FRANKFURT

Frankfurt is at the crossroads of Germany where transportation routes converge. If you have the inclination to visit the heart of this modern vibrant metropolis, venture downtown to explore the modern core and be sure to include a visit to the house where Johann Wolfgang von Goethe spent his formative years. If you do not want to go into the city yet are looking for an idyllic spot to rest and recover from the rigors of transatlantic jetlag before beginning your sightseeing, the Schloss Kronberg is an elegant, expensive, luxury hotel within a half hour's drive of Frankfurt's busy airport.

DESTINATION I   BAD HERSFELD   Hotel Zum Stern

Leaving Frankfurt, take the autobahn 5 north for about an hour and a half to ALSFELD. The town's lovely historic core is not large and is easily explored on foot. The town hall is raised above the square by tall stone arches which gave the citizens of old a sheltered place to hold their market day. This half-timbered building, with its peaked turrets looking like witches' hats, is one of the finest in Germany. Explore the streets around the market square for they are full of old leaning houses and cobbles worn smooth by many feet over the centuries.   Because of its historic old buildings, the town was chosen to receive a facelift in 1975 to celebrate European Architectural Heritage Year.

The area around Alsfeld is known as Red Riding Hood country.   When the Grimm brothers collected their fairytales they noted that the young girls of the area wore small red cloaks with hoods, and hence the title to the story.   At festival times you will see young girls in their traditional costumes topped by small red cloaks.

Romantik Hotel Zum Stern
Bad Hersfeld

Following road 62 to the east, about an hour's drive through pretty countryside brings you to the town of BAD HERSFELD.   Bad Hersfeld is rather plain in comparison to some of the towns you will see - but handsome none the less.   At its heart lies a large market square lined with old burghers' houses.   Part of the square has been turned into a pedestrian mall and it is in this pedestrian zone, with its tables and chairs spilling over into the square, that you will find the HOTEL

ZUM STERN. Bustling and welcoming, the inn has been offering hospitality to weary travelers for over 500 years. Try to secure one of the darling rooms at the front of the hotel: with their blackened beams, creaking floorboards and antique furniture, they are a real prize.

Your location on the market square is ideal for exploring. Thankfully the town is not a tourist trap, but a busy assortment of everyday shops - butchers and grocers plus wonderful cafes offering coffee and mouth-watering pastries. Admire the architecture of the houses in the old town and do not miss the majestic ruined abbey which makes a splendid backdrop for the famous musical festival held here every July.

It is said that George III of England enlisted many Bad Hersfeld soldiers to help put down the American Revolution - the poor men were so terrified by a dreadful Atlantic crossing that those who survived the war stayed put in America.

DESTINATION II   SABABURG   Burghotel Sababurg

When it is time to leave Bad Hersfeld take the road 27 to the north through BEBRA where you turn left on the road 83 for the short drive to ROTENBERG AN DER FULDA. As you turn into this old town you will see ancient houses sheltered beneath the cliff which rises dramatically from the River Fulda.

Next, follow country roads north for the short drive to SPANGENBERG. Stroll amidst the old houses on the town's main street, the Klosterstrasse, and then drive up the winding road to the SCHLOSS SPANGENBERG that looms above the town. From the castle ramparts the tiny brown and black timbered houses of the town below look as if they belong in a child's toy box. If the weather is fine, the restaurant on the ramparts makes a perfect refreshment stop: the town is spread before you and the castle rises steeply to your back.

Continue to the north through the town of HESSISCH LICHTENAU for the short drive to KASSEL. The town has centuries of history but is now modern in style largely because the Allies flattened most of it during World War II. This modern sprawling metropolis is the heart of German fairytale country for it was here that the great folklorists Jakob and Wilhelm Grimm worked as court librarians between 1805 and 1830. In their spare time the congenial brothers walked the countryside collecting myths, legends and folktales. Pausing for a glass of beer at the Knallhutte (brewery) in the nearby town of BAUNATAL, they met Dorothea Viehmann, an old lady with a passion for yarns. She was born at the brewery and over the years had picked up stories from travelers. The brothers were attentive listeners and even better writers: in 1815 they published a collection of their tales that is known the world over as "Grimm's Fairy Tales". If you are interested in their writing, you will want to visit the "Brudder-Grimm Museum" with its memorabilia of their lives and works: it is well marked from the center of town. Otherwise it is best to avoid Kassel's urban sprawl and let the autobahn whisk you northwards to HANN MUNDEN.

Where the Weser and the Werra rivers converge, the town of Hann Munden has grown, a town of graceful old houses embellished with figures, animal heads and curlicues. Walking along some of the old side streets, you will notice the fronts of the houses look like the prows of a fleet of old galleons leaning against the wind. The old town has survived turbulent centuries intact - all that has been needed is a touchup coat of paint here and there. The eccentric "quack" Dr Eisenbart is buried in the town. In the 17th century he was a successful surgeon and doctor - although his doctoring was somewhat unorthodox: "I give back the blind the use of their legs, the paralyzed their sight, I give shots in the middle of the stitch, for anesthesia I use ten pounds of opium." Apparently proud of its rather unorthodox surgeon, the town honors him with summer performances of the play "Dr Eisenbart".

Follow the River Weser to the north as it leaves Hann Munden. A left turn in the nearby village of REINHARDSHAGEN takes you through the "enchanted" forest of the Rheinhard to your hotel for tonight, the BURGHOTEL SABABURG, more often referred to as Sleeping Beauty's Castle. The Brothers Grimm visited Sababurg Castle and used it as the setting for their famous story. Plan on arriving late in the day to avoid the coachloads of daytime tourists that flock to this attraction.

Burghotel Sababurg
Sababurg

What was once a proud fortress is now largely a romantic ruin - a shell of towers and walls. Fortunately one wing has been restored as a hotel. The dining room serves superb venison and provides lovely views of the countryside and distant forest. There is no lounge or bar to gather in before or after dinner, so splurge and request a larger room. The romance of staying in Sleeping Beauty's castle cannot be denied, but be aware that the castle is very isolated.

Bid farewell to Sleeping Beauty's domain and retrace your steps into the forest taking the road north to the Weser River. Cross the river and follow signs that lead you east to USLAR, an enchanting town of many half-timbered houses.

From Uslar it is about a 45-minute drive to GOTTINGEN, an old university town where the Brothers Grimm taught. Apart from admiring its old and very lovely architecture, you must visit Liesel, the goose girl, whose statue stands atop the fountain in front of the town hall on the market square. She is reputed to be the most kissed girl in the world. This is no small surprise for the story says that anyone who kisses Liesel will enjoy good luck the rest of his life.

Romantik Hotel Zur Tanne
Braunlage

Leaving Gottingen, main roads take you east for the half-hour drive to HERZBERG located at the foot of the HARZ MOUNTAINS. From Herzberg, continue east upwards into the mountains to ST ANDREASBURG. High atop a hill, the town's streets drop steeply to the old Samson Silver Mine in the valley.

Since the mine closed in 1910, the little town has become an attractive tourist center.

A few miles beyond St Andreasburg, tucked close to the East German border, is BRAUNLAGE. On the town's main street you will find the small ROMANTIK HOTEL ZUR TANNE. The owners, Helmut and Barbel Herbst, are perfect hosts, whose warm welcome, excellent English and concern for their guests' comfort add to an enjoyable stay. The large dining room is the center of activity for the hotel and has gained a well deserved reputation for fine cuisine and excellent service. The choice bedrooms are found at the front; cozy little rooms in the tiny old section of the hotel.

DESTINATION IV   GOSLAR   Hotel Kaiserworth

Reflecting the state of Germany's division, the border between East and West Germany runs through the Harz Mountains: much of the mountain range lies temptingly out of reach across the border. What remains in Western Germany is yours to explore: wild mountain scenery that never runs out of interest, deep gullies, tumbling mountain streams, green forests, and cool blue lakes - ideal country for hiking in the summer and cross country skiing in the winter.

The Brothers Grimm did not come this far north and thus missed a myth that was saved for Goethe who used it as a basis for the witches' sabbath in "Faust". It is said that on Walpurgisnacht, April 30th, cackling witches astride their broomsticks gather on the summit of Mount Brocken to cavort and cast their wicked spells.

As the itinerary's final destination lies only 25 miles north, take the opportunity for some leisurely sightseeing of this lovely region. Buy a walking map of the area and combine today's sightseeing with a walk to one of the lakes whose warm summer surfaces welcome swimmers but whose depths remain icy cold.

Leave Braunlage driving north along road 4, skirting the Harz's highest mountain, the Brocken, whose summit lies in East Germany. In TORFHAUS, the busy small tourist center for the mountains, turn left along the Altenau road: the views of the valleys are quite breathtaking along this narrow road. In the ski resort of ALTENAU, bear left along road 498 and shortly right along road 242. As the road descends into CLAUSTHAL-ZELLERFELD you have beautiful views across forested high mountain valleys to East Germany.

The twin towns of Clausthal and Zellerfeld were the capital of the Harz mining region, and the Oberharzer Museum in Zellerfeld is dedicated to mining in the Harz. Apart from displays of rock specimens and old-fashioned mining paraphernalia, rooms have been set up to give you a glimpse of eras long past showing how the miners lived and worked. Leaving the first museum, you cross a rustic courtyard and enter a mock-up of an old-fashioned underground mine. Here, as you wind up and down through the tunnels, a venerable old miner gives a discourse in German. It is all very self-explanatory so do not worry if you understand not a word.

Just on the southern outskirts of Zellerfeld, take the road to the right to SCHULENBERG and the OKER DAM. The road traces the dam and, as the valley narrows, follows the Oker river as it cascades and tumbles down from the mountains to the plain below. Linger in this wild and romantic river valley, an understandable favorite of visitors to the Harz.

Saving the best for last, you come to the capital of the region, the old imperial town of GOSLAR. Ambling through the town past half-timbered houses on crooked streets is like taking a walk back into the Middle Ages. The River Gose tumbles through the town past quaint red-tiled houses to the majestic 11th-century imperial palace, once the largest non-church building in the empire.

Occupying a corner of the market square, the old town merchants' guildhall is now the HOTEL KAISERWORTH where statues of German emperors guard the portals. Here you are only steps away from the town's main sights: the town hall, the market church and the Goslarer Museum with its fascinating displays of life in old Goslar. Step outside your hotel at six in the evening and watch the concert of the city clock whose four different scenes represent the 1,000-year-old mining history of the region. In such a colorful town, it is no wonder the bedrooms overlooking the market square are so popular with guests.

Hotel Kaiserworth
Goslar

Leaving Goslar, it is only a few miles to the autobahn where you have the choice of going south to Frankfurt, north to Hamburg or east to Berlin.

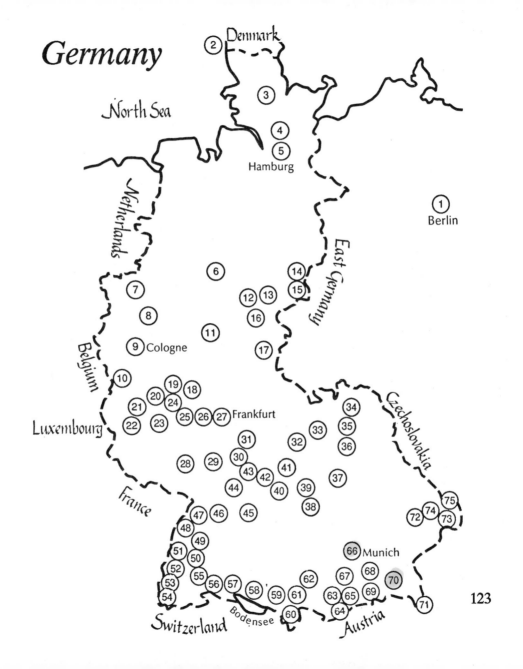

Germany

Denmark

North Sea

Netherlands

Hamburg

East Germany

Berlin

Cologne

Belgium

Luxembourg

Frankfurt

Czechoslovakia

France

Munich

Switzerland

Bodensee

Austria

123

If you are looking for an isolated hideaway far from the oft' trod tourist paths, the Hotel Topferhaus fits the bill. Hugging the shores of the tranquil Bisten lake, surrounded by manicured gardens, the Hotel Topferhaus commands a serene setting. The building is a squat whitewashed farmhouse topped by a broad thatch roof. The airy interior is packed with lovely antiques highlighted by country accents and Oriental rugs. The owners, the Brammer family, have a real eye for beautiful beds, armoirs and chests. The majority of the bedrooms have captivating views of the Bistensee gently lapping at the lawn in front of the hotel. You can enjoy the same spectacular lake view in the adjacent elegant Restaurant Topferhaus. In addition, several bedrooms have the homey comfort of adjacent sitting areas with deep comfortable chairs and writing bureaus. The dining room at the hotel serves only breakfast. German is the only language spoken at the hotel. The Topferhaus is quite difficult to find: take the autobahn 7 north from Hamburg to the Rendsburg exit, then as you leave the autobahn, turn right and a few minutes' drive brings you the tiny village of Holzbunge. Turn left through the village and you will find the hotel just a short drive away on the shore of the Bistensee.

HOTEL TOPFERHAUS
Owner: Family Brammer
2371 Alt Duvenstedt, Germany
Tel: (04338) 333
16 Rooms
Sgl from 76 DM Dbl to 157 DM
Open: All year
Elegant antique furniture
Beautiful lakeside setting
Located 140 km N of Hamburg

On a hillside dotted with grazing sheep, near the village of Amorbach, is Der Schafhof, one of Germany's loveliest hotels. Built in 1721, it originally belonged to the estate of the Amorbach Benedictine Abbey. Now the flag bearing the crest of the Winkler family who were once the titled millers of the region is proudly raised out front. Der Schafhof is still an operating farm with sheep, goats, hens and ducks, but the Winkler family also provide excellent accommodations and cuisine. There are only sixteen rooms in the hotel, thirteen with private bath: the decor is consistently beautiful with a theme of natural dyes in tones of brown, cream and white. Decorated in warm colors with soft lighting, lovely flower arrangements and intimately placed tables, the restaurant is captivating. The cuisine is exceptional and the wine cellar boasts an excellent selection of regional wines. Space is provided in the stables for guests' horses. Der Schafhof also has horse-drawn sleighs for country rides through snow or across lush green farmland and there are miles of undeveloped land to explore. A very handsome couple, the Winklers afford travelers a splendid retreat.

DER SCHAFHOF
Owner: Dr Winkler
8762 Amorbach, Germany
Tel: (09373) 8088, telex: 689293 amot
16 Rooms
Sgl from 125 DM Dbl to 250 DM
Closed: January and February
Credit Cards: All major
Tennis
Located 80 km SE of Frankfurt

Assmannshausen is a lovely little village on the Rhine, relatively unspoilt by any overabundance of postcard or tourist shops, as is the unfortunate case in nearby Rudesheim. Its scenic main street along the river offers several hotels, but the best bargain for the location is the Hotel Anker. Wisteria winds around the arched windows on the ground floor of this cheerful yellow hotel. Built in 1666 by Johann Jung, the Hotel Anker is still owned and managed with much pride by the Jung family. Guests are warmly welcomed into this charming hotel by Herr Jung who speaks good English, as well as French and Italian. The Anker's restaurant has two inviting dining rooms with dark beamed ceilings, rose tablecloths and a collection of old prints, paintings and pewter. The splendid view of the Rhine is seen from all tables through the large windows framed by pretty forest green and rose print drapes. The menu here offers an imaginative variety of dishes complemented by the special wines produced in the area. The 50 bedrooms all have clean private baths and are tastefully furnished with contemporary furnishings, flowered wallpaper and pictures on the walls. A few antique pieces adorn the halls and a beautiful old stained glass window is found on the stairwell. This comfortable hotel is recommended for its charm, value, and solicitous host.

HOTEL ANKER
Owner: Family Jung
Rheinuferstrasse 5
6224 Assmannshausen am Rhein, Germany
Tel: (06722) 2912
50 Rooms
Sgl from 68 DM Dbl to 128 DM
Closed: mid November to February
Credit Cards: MC, VS
Elevator
Located 60 km W of Frankfurt

The tiny wine village of Assmannshausen has grown up at a slight widening of the narrow Rhine river gorge.   Limited by its geographic location, the village has not been spoiled by modern development and remains as a cramped cluster of old houses overlooking the river.   Fronting the Rhine river, the Hotel Krone has been providing bed, food and drink to weary travelers since 1541.   The hotel's vine-covered terrace and raised restaurant provide lovely places for dining while watching the busy river life slide by.   Much of the building dates from the turn of the century.   The interior is perfectly in keeping with the exterior, with large, rather heavy, pieces of lovingly polished furniture against dark paneled walls. Since the hotel is sandwiched between the railroad tracks and the river, you will get the best night's sleep by requesting a river-facing room in the hotel annex.   Hotel rooms in the main building are more charming but their toilets are always across the hall.   Rhine river steamers arrive and depart from the dock just a five-minute walk away: if you arrive by boat the hotel will gladly send someone to meet you and tend to your luggage.   Located on a lovely section of the Rhine, the hotel provides an ideal base for exploring the river and the surrounding Rheingau wine area.

HOTEL KRONE
Owner: Family Hufnagel
6620 Assmannshausen, Germany
Tel: (06722) 2036
82 Rooms
Sgl from 107 DM Dbl to 224 DM
Open: mid March to mid November
Credit Cards: All major
Beautiful Rhine River setting
Located 60 km W of Frankfurt

Come dream a romantic dream or two in this imposing hillside fortress. Surrounded by dense forest, the Burg Schnellenberg has been around since 1255. Over the years it has been altered, added to and finally restored into an elegant castle hotel. The halls display enormous old oil paintings. The bedrooms vary in their size and aspect: you may find yourself in a cozy paneled room with a window seat overlooking the trout ponds or high atop a winding turret staircase in a room with twenty-foot-high ceilings and a lofty view over the surrounding countryside. The furniture is large and old, not as old as the castle but very old none the less. The main dining room is splendid: several rooms with lofty ceilings, an enormous old tapestry decorating the main wall, and groupings of elegant tables and chairs. A further dining room is decorated in a hunting lodge motif and beneath it lies a cozy wine cellar bar. Other cellars comprise a museum where rows of cases are filled with weapons and suits of armor. Tucked away in the upper castle is a 17th century family chapel whose vaulted ceiling is covered with decorative biblical frescoes.

BURGHOTEL SCHNELLENBERG
Owner: Family Bilsing
5952 Attendorn, Germany
Tel: (02722) 6940
Telex: 876732
45 Rooms
Sgl from 70 DM Dbl to 210 DM
Open: end January to mid December
Credit Cards: AX, DC
Wonderful hilltop castle
Located 170 km E of Cologne

A stay at the Brauerei-Gasthof-Hotel Aying is a country German experience not soon to be forgotten. It is a famous brewery, restaurant and hotel all rolled into one typically Bavarian package. The hotel's wisteria-covered facade is easily spotted thanks to a giant, blue-striped flagpole in the front yard. The front doors and entry area are painted a bright blue, complemented by many painted flowers and German proverbs inscribed on the ceiling beams. Fresh flowers and large dried flower arrangements abound in all the public areas, and traditional "hearts and flowers" painting adorns most every nook and cranny; on armoires, beams, staircases and old chests. The restaurant offers candlelit dinners in front of a large, open fireplace. The romantic scene is completed with Dutch blue tablecloths set with shining china and glassware. Traditional Bavarian specialties of ham and pork, and of course all varieties of the famous Aying beer are offered with pride. Upstairs, the 19 guest bedrooms are furnished with farm style furniture and all but two have private baths which are very clean, though not extremely modern. The brewery town of Aying is a small, rural village, where the Hotel Aying offers friendly, Bavarian style hospitality, removed from the traffic jams and crowds of Munich.

BRAUEREI-GASTHOF-HOTEL AYING
Owner: Family Inselkammer
8011 Aying bei Munchen, Germany
Tel: (08095) 705
19 Rooms
Sgl from 80 DM Dbl to 165 DM
Closed: January 2 to February 1
Credit Cards: AX, MC, DC
Brewery
Located 20 km SE of Munich

With its soft yellow facade covered in draping wisteria, the Hotel Zum Hirsch enjoys a delightful location at the heart of the pedestrian zone of Baden-Baden. Tucked in a corner just off the principal cobbled street, its neighbors are elegant shops, boutiques and restaurants that are sought by a very particular and international crowd. Associated for the past two years with and managed by the larger, very elegant Steigenburger Badischer Hof Hotel, the Hotel Zum Hirsch is smaller, run on more personal lines without sacrificing quality, facilities or elegance. Built in 1689, this is the oldest hotel in town and the Zum Hirsch prides itself as one of the two establishments in town to have its own thermal well. The reception area is small and modern and the staff welcoming and fluent in English. The bar, set directly off the lobby, is handsome in browns, with a few well placed antiques. The bedrooms are very comfortable in size, attractively furnished and all have bathrooms equipped with thermal water. The hotel has a lovely restaurant and offers a pension package in addition to a bountiful buffet breakfast.

HOTEL ZUM HIRSCH
Manager: Klaus Fischer
Hirschstrasse 1
7570 Baden-Baden, Germany
Tel: (07221) 23896 telex: 781193
59 Rooms
Sgl from 110 DM Dbl to 189 DM
Credit Cards: All major
Swimming pool
Located 275 km S of Frankfurt

I postponed writing the description of the Hotel Sonne, not because of the task, but out of a desire to make the description the best it could be - to do justice to the excellence of the hotel and the hospitality and character of its owner. Herr Fischer continues a tradition begun by his grandfather some hundred years ago, a hotel where guests are welcomed year after year, where a sense of home is created. This is the oldest gasthaus in Badenweiler and Herr Fischer has a greeting and a loving smile for all.   He and his wife are ever present among their guests, selecting wines, suggesting outings or escorting excursions themselves. A walk into the surrounding Black Forest or an outing to Alsace for a little wine are better for their company.   Very caring hosts, the Fischers offer accommodations of comfort that vary from simple rooms to beautiful traditional to very commodious apartments. Of the restaurants, one is cozy and intimate, and a larger, more formal, dining room is for pension guests.   The Fischer family once also had vineyards but now Herr Fischer is dedicated solely to the hotel business and it shows.

ROMANTIK HOTEL SONNE
Owner: Mr & Mrs Fischer
7847 Badenweiler, Germany
Tel: (07632) 5053
55 Rooms
Sgl from 75 DM Dbl to 175 DM
Open: February 9 to November 16
Credit Cards: All major
U.S. Rep: Romantik Hotels
Rep. tel: 800-826-0015
Located 46 km S of Freiburg

Bamberg is a beautiful town and a destination that deserves more attention than given in travel literature. From a distance, the six spires of its church pierce the skyline. At its center, Bamberg is a complex of quaint cobbled pedestrian streets, outdoor cafes, bridges and enchanting houses that grace and line the waterfront. Not more than a few blocks from the old section of town is a simple hotel and wonderful restaurant - the Romantik Hotel Weinhaus Messerschmitt. The hotel has only twelve rooms for overnight guests but a restaurant that is sought by many. The bedrooms are found up a marvelous wooden handcarved stairway and are identified from other offices and private rooms by hanging, numbered wine bottles. The bedrooms are simple but sweet in decor. Down comforters deck the beds and the bathroom facilities are modern but enhanced by lovely old fixtures. At night it is difficult to shut out the street noise but a welcome cognac left by the considerate management might be all you need to sleep.

ROMANTIK WEINHAUS MESSERSCHMITT
Owner: Otto Pschorn
Lange Strasse 41
8600 Bamberg, Germany
Tel: (0951) 27866
12 Rooms
Sgl from 68 DM Dbl to 157 DM
Open: All year
Credit Cards: All major
U.S. Rep: Romantik Hotels
Rep. tel: 800-826-0015
Located 230 km N of Munich

Set a country road's distance from the city of Bayreuth is a lovely castle hotel where one is treated more as "royalty" than simply as "Gast im Schloss". Intimate in its size, the Jagdschloss Thiergarten is an old hunting castle that has converted nine rooms to accommodate overnight guests. You can retire to a bedchamber and then choose from one of two lovely dining rooms. The Kamin Restaurant is small with just a few elegantly set tables warmed by a dramatic fireplace, and hence its name: "Kamin" translates as fireplace. The Venezianischer Salon's focus is on a very intricate Venetian glass chandelier that dates back approximately 300 years. The Barocksaal, used for banquets or weddings, is found in the imposing rotunda, open to a detailed ceiling and second floor balcony. When the hotel was a hunting lodge, guests actually shot from the vantage point of the balcony. In warm weather tables are set out on a stretch of grass behind the castle, under the blossoms of cherry and apple trees. The bedrooms are furnished appropriately for an old fortress, handsome in furnishings but a bit worn. Open as a hotel for approximately 40 years, the Schloss Hotel Thiergarten provides a lovely retreat from the neighboring city of Bayreuth.

SCHLOSS HOTEL THIERGARTEN
Owner: Kaiser Harald
8580 Bayreuth, Germany
Tel: (09209) 1314
9 Rooms
Sgl from 74 DM Dbl to 126 DM
Open: All year
Credit Cards: All major
Located 230 km N of Munich

This is certainly an old family business: Mrs Lipmann, her son Goachim and her daughter Marion are the sixth and seventh generations of the family to run this inn and tend the family vineyards that rise steeply above the banks of the Moselle river. This small hotel is especially appealing because it is located at the heart of the prettiest village along the Moselle. With its picturesque medieval buildings, church and ruined castle, Beilstein is a gem. The dining rooms are just as quaint as the exterior: you may find yourself in a small farmhouse-style room before an old fireplace, in the warm paneled main dining room or feasting in the knights' hall surrounded by collections of old weapons. When weather permits, you can move out of doors to the terrace and watch the life on the gentle Moselle river glide by as you dine, then wind your way up through the narrow cobbled streets to enjoy the view from the church before returning to the square for a glass of wine in the 400-year-old wine cellar. None of the guest rooms offer much charm, but the rooms in the old inn have more appeal than those in the modern annex set amongst the vineyard. The two "choice" rooms have balconies and river views. Additional very simple rooms are found in a house next to the river road. The town's wine festival takes place during the first weekend in September.

HOTEL HAUS LIPMANN
Owner: Family Lipmann
5591 Beilstein, Germany
Tel: (02673) 1573
25 Rooms
Sgl from 74 DM Dbl to 79 DM
Open: April to October
Along the Moselle River
Located 150 km NW of Frankfurt

The Hotel Geiger is a large mountain cabin with the elegance of a fine city hotel. Set on the hillside on the outskirts of Berchtesgaden in the direction of Bad Reichenall, the hotel is a weathered chalet attractively decked with green shutters, wooden balconies and overflowing flower boxes. With its traditional Bavarian decor, the Hotel Geiger blends perfectly into this Alpine region on the Austrian-Swiss border. The entrance into the main building exposes the richness of a wood-paneled dining room with handsome painted ceilings, planked floors, heart-carved chairs, red print cushions, Oriental carpets, hand carved figurine chandeliers, pewter, candles, antlers and the peaceful background of ticking old clocks - an atmosphere reminiscent of one of Scotland's finest hunting lodges. A sitting area adjoins the restaurant and its decor is consistent in rich tones and quality. Like a private library, the salon is warmed by an open fire, with heavy fabrics, wood paneling and large windows opening onto Alpine views. There are forty rooms in the old house and ten in a neighboring new annex. All the rooms enjoy views of the mountains.

HOTEL GEIGER
Owner: Hugo Geiger
Stanggasse
8240 Berchtesgaden, Germany
Tel: (08652) 5055 telex: 56222
50 Rooms
Sgl from 130 DM Dbl to 300 DM
Open: All year
Credit Cards: AX, EC, DC
Swimming pool
Located 154 km SE of Munich

The atmospheric Hotel Watzmann is centrally located in Berchtesgaden across from the Franziskaner Kirche on the main road through town. It was originally built as a beer brewery in the 1600s and is now a family-run hotel filled with antiques, memorabilia and charm. The yellow facade with its green shutters and bright red geraniums is set back from the road behind a large terrace filled with tables, umbrellas, and, on a warm day, many patrons. The public areas and two dining rooms contain plenty of old prints, painted antique furniture and hunting trophies, as well as beamed ceilings and old ceramic stoves. Menu selections are traditionally Bavarian, featuring delicious pork and game dishes. The hotel has 38 bedrooms, only 17 of which have private baths, and none of which are equipped with phones or televisions. Bedrooms are comfortable, clean, and well appointed with reproduction Bavarian style furniture, and large family suites are also available. The upstairs hallways are decorated by door panels painted with Bavarian floral designs and a collection of colorful old archery targets. Antique chests, armoires, and paintings are also displayed in abundance. This is a very warm Bavarian inn, owned and managed with personal care by the English speaking Piscantor family.

HOTEL WATZMANN
Owner: Family Hinrich Piscantor
Franziskanerplatz
8240 Berchtesgaden, Germany
Tel: (08652) 2055
38 Rooms
Sgl from 25 DM Dbl to 96 DM
Closed: October 15 to December 23
Credit Cards: None
Restaurant, Parking
Located 120 km SE of Munich, near the Austrian border

Elly Lange owns and manages the Pension Dittberner and lovingly tends to the needs of her guests. The atmosphere is homey and her guests consider this their home in Berlin. Located on a quiet side street just off the surging Kurfurstendamm, you enter into a dimly lit lobby and climb long flights of stairs to the third floor. Thankfully this need only be done once as Elly will give you a key to the charming old-fashioned elevator and explain its mysterious workings to you. An elaborate chandelier graces the lobby-lounge where guests gather to discuss and plan their sightseeing. Discussions continue in the adjacent breakfast room whose large Oriental rug and chandelier add an elegant touch. The walls and hallways display Elly's eclectic art collection, from Javan puppets to French posters and a modern sculpture or two for good measure. The bedrooms are freshly painted in bright shades: the furnishings plain with white linens and plump eiderdowns on the beds. Twelve rooms have showers with toilets across the hall, while the four choice rooms have private bathrooms. This bed and breakfast inn far outshines the other small hotels that I visited in Berlin.

PENSION DITTBERNER
Owner: Mrs Elly Lange
Wielandstrasse 26
1000 Berlin, Germany
Tel: (030) 881 6485
20 Rooms
Sgl from 57 DM Dbl to 115 DM
Open: All year
Charming pension
Located in the city center

The Hotel Am Zoo has an excellent location at the center of Kurfurstendamm. Lined with shops and cafes, this is the street at the heart of Berlin, humming with activity twenty-four hours a day. You step from the bustling crowds into the peace and quiet of the hotel's maple-lined lobby, from which a gleaming glass elevator whisks you to your room. The hotel's most unusual aspect is the elevator shaft which has been painted as a mural of trees and greenery. The bedrooms are small, modern and blissfully quiet, for all are soundproofed to prevent the intrusion of street noise. A quarter of the rooms face the Kurfurstendamm and, while it is fun to watch the crowds below, blinds have been thoughtfully provided to eliminate the bright city lights. A delicious buffet-style breakast is served in the hotel dining room. Berlin abounds with large, modern hotels, and the style of the Am Zoo makes a refreshing change from these concrete giants. Although the staff does not seem to radiate much warmth, the hotel has a perfect location at the heart of Berlin.

HOTEL AM ZOO
Owner: Mr Uohler
Kurfurstendamm 25
1000 Berlin, Germany
Tel: (03088) 3091 telex: 183835
142 Rooms
Sgl from 103 DM Dbl to 179 DM
Open: All year
Credit Cards: All major
Garage parking available
Located in the city center

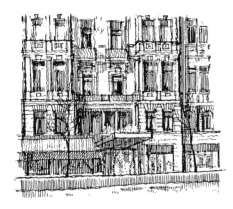

Bernkastel is the most charming of the larger towns along the Moselle. Fronting the river are large turn-of-the-century hotels, but venture behind them and you find winding, cobblestoned streets lined by 400-year-old half-timbered houses. In amongst these side streets is found the Doctor Weinstuben. Named after the local tax collector, Doctor Wein, who lived here in the 17th century, the house went on to become a wine room and in 1974 became a hotel when a modern block of rooms was built across the courtyard. While an effort was made to put an olde worlde exterior on the annex, the accommodations are modern, functional hotel rooms. Their decor is clean and bright but far from memorable. Each room has a private bathroom. By sharp contrast, the hotel has put a great deal of effort into making the restaurant in the old wine room reflect the atmosphere of this pretty little wine town. A large hay wagon stands as a decorative centerpiece and around it the lofty room has been divided into intimate dining nooks with beams and dark wood.

HOTEL DOCTOR WEINSTUBEN
Hebegasse 5
5550 Bernkastel, Germany
Tel: (06531) 6081
15 Rooms
Sgl from 70 DM Dbl to 125 DM
Open: January to October
Credit Cards: All major
Lovely River Moselle town
Located 75 km SW of Koblenz

The Hotel Zur Post is lovingly and professionally looked after by owners Frau and Herr Rossling. True hoteliers, the Rosslings do a superb job and are always striving to improve their charming hotel. Located slightly away from the center of town and right on the banks of the Moselle, the Zur Post has a mustard colored facade which is complemented by dark green shutters and windowboxes of red geraniums. In the oldest part of the Zur Post, dating from 1827, guests climb a narrow old stairway to rooms which do not all have private baths, but are spotlessly clean. A new annex has recently been added to the hotel, but so skillfully done that from the exterior the entire ensemble looks original. The newer rooms combine modern appointments with tasteful decorating, adding up to a level of comfort that is truly a treat. The Zur Post's excellent kitchen serves a generous breakfast buffet as well as savory lunch and dinner specialties. Guests may choose to dine in any one of the three warm dining rooms. The informal restaurant has walls and ceilings entirely of carved pine complemented by dried flower arrangements and bright tablecloths. Usually full of fun-loving guests, the restaurant is also a cozy spot for an afternoon sampling of the crisp, white regional wines. The other two dining rooms offer a slightly more refined atmosphere with tableside service and attentive waiters

HOTEL ZUR POST
Owner: Family Rossling
5550 Bernkastel, Germany
Tel: (06531) 2022
39 Rooms
Sgl from 45 DM Dbl to 130 DM
Open: All year
Credit Cards: All major
Lovely River Moselle town
Located 75 km SW of Koblenz

The Storzer family have lovingly converted a building that dates from 1500 and added an annex to offer guests 27 delightful rooms in a village whose inhabitants probably number even fewer than the guests in the hotel. In this rural setting mornings might be disturbed by the sound of milkcarts or a tractor. The Romantik Hotel Bierhutte incorporates the Bavarian theme throughout in its decor. Stenciling, found bordering doorways, is used to identify rooms, and furnishings are in light wood enhanced by lovely handpainted designs - so typical of the region. All the rooms in the new annex have either a balcony or terrace depending on whether they are found on the ground or first floor and the entire basement of the annex is devoted to a playroom equipped with toys, sauna, solarium, ping pong table and fitness room. In the main building, the restaurant, "Wappenstupen", is named for the coats of armor displayed on the walls, the "Gaststube" is a cozy room available for either a meal or refreshment, and the cheery breakfast room benefits from the morning sun. A lovely terrace, overlooking the lake, is used on warmer days for dining.

ROMANTIK HOTEL BIERHUTTE
Owner: Family Storzer
8351 Bierhutte, Germany
Tel: (08558) 315 telex: 57446
27 Rooms
Sgl from 70 DM Dbl to 140 DM
Open: All year
Credit Cards: DC, AX
U.S. Rep: Romantik Hotels
Rep. tel: 800-826-0015
Located 205 km N of Munich

A wonderfully rustic, country home atmosphere prevails at the Landhotel Schindlerhof. A recently renovated and enlarged farm complex, it is built around a large open courtyard where tables are set in summer for cocktails and evening barbecues. Inside, the two dining rooms are "country cozy", yet also retain a certain elegance. The walls and ceilings are warm knotty pine, matched by light pine furniture throughout. Hanging baskets, shafts of harvest wheat, dried and fresh flowers brighten all corners of the rooms, while charming rose and white checked tablecloths are complemented by lace curtains and pink candles. Waitresses are introduced by name, and are all attired in pretty, traditional dirndls. The menu is imaginative and varied, offering cosmopolitan gourmet selections as well as fresh, health-food entrees. In all areas of the Schindlerhof, host Klaus Kobjoll's attention to the smallest detail is infallible. From thoughtful touches such as welcoming fruit baskets in each guest bedroom, packets of German "gummi bears" underneath the pillows, to a complimentary glass of sherry or champagne upon arrival, every comfort is attended to.   Guest bedrooms are all fresh and new, but never sterile.   Light pine antique reproductions furnish the spacious rooms, all of which have a pine writing table, good lighting, discreet color television, minibar, and telephone.

LANDHOTEL SCHINDLERHOF
Owner: Family Kobjoll
8500 Nurnberg-Boxdorf, Germany
Tel: (0911) 302077 telex: 179118619
30 Rooms
Sgl from 89 DM Dbl to 165 DM
Open: All year
Credit Cards: All major
Free bicycle rental
Located 10 km from Nurnberg, 3.5 km from airport

The little town of Braubach lies on the Rhine almost opposite Koblenz. In amongst a mixture of modern and old houses you find the Zum Weissen Schwanen leaning against the old city wall where the large tower extends into the street. Step behind the half-timbered facade and you enter a gem of a country rustic tavern: warm pine paneling, bottle-glass dimpled windows hung with hand-crocheted curtains, and simple pine tables and carved chairs. Your genial hosts, Erich and Gerhilde Kunz, will probably be there to welcome you. Although they speak but a few words of English, their warm smiles and exuberant gestures overcome any language barrier. A few bedrooms are found in the converted stables behind the tavern. While these are charming, the inn's choice rooms lie in a nearby watermill where a huge wooden waterwheel slowly turns at the building's center. Around the waterwheel passages and staircases lead to the bedchambers. The bedrooms are a country delight - rustic handicrafts surround old pine beds topped with plump gingham pillows and comforters. The Kunz family has a restaurant at the heart of the mill. The hotel gives you a wonderful feel of days gone by. There is nothing pretentious about the Zum Weissen Schwanen: it is just an old-fashioned inn in a picturesque, but non-touristy, town run with great pride by very nice people.

HOTEL ZUM WEISSEN SCHWANEN
Owner: Erich Kunz
Brunnenstr 4
5423 Braubach, Germany
Tel: (02627) 559
14 Rooms
Sgl from 40 DM Dbl to 95 DM
Open: All year
Lovely old watermill
Located 130 km NW of Frankfurt

Hotel Descriptions   143

You will have no problem finding the Romantik Hotel Zur Tanne; its pretty little facade graces the town's main street. Probably one of your genial hosts, Helmut and Barbel Herbst, will be there to greet you. Their warm welcome, excellent English and concern for their guests' comfort add to an enjoyable stay. From a tiny entrance the hotel opens up to reveal a large dignified dining room. This is the center of activity, for the hotel has gained a well-deserved reputation for excellent meals and impeccable service. Up the winding front staircase you find a few country-cozy bedrooms. I suggest you request one of these when making a reservation. A wing of modern rooms, decorated in shades of green, stretches out from the rear of the old inn. The hotel's most rustic room is its cheery bar where guests gather for after-dinner drinks and discussions of the day's events. Budget travelers can find more simple accommodations at the Guesthouse Zur Tanne on the edge of town. The surrounding countryside is lovely, for Braunlage is in the heart of the Harz Mountains. In summer there is beautiful scenery to explore and winter offers the opportunity for cross-country skiing.

ROMANTIK HOTEL ZUR TANNE
Owner: Helmut and Barbel Herbst
3389 Braunlage, Germany
Tel: (05520) 1034/5
21 Rooms
Sgl from 80 DM Dbl to 175 DM
Open: All year
Credit Cards: All major
U.S. Rep: Romantik Hotels
Rep. tel: 800-826-0015
Harz Mountain village
Located 275 km S of Hamburg

The Alte Rheinmuhle is in a little niche of Germany, practically surrounded by Switzerland, only 2 1/2 miles east of Schaffhausen. The distance between the countries is so short and the town so Swiss that customs are friendly and casual although you do need your passport to cross the border. The Alte Rheinmuhle is truly a wonderful transformation of an old mill to functioning inn and accomplished with delightful taste. The building dates from 1674 and sits right on the edge of the Rhine. On the first floor is a beautiful dining room whose large windows overlook the river. The hotel has earned an outstanding reputation for its cuisine and extensive wine cellar. Some of the restaurant's specialties include superb venison and wild rabbit, and the highlight for dessert is the most scrumptious cassis sherbet to be found anywhere. I discussed the rooms with the management and was told that all rooms are decorated in a country style and furnished with antiques - some even have four-poster beds. Our room, number fourteen, with twin beds, is set under old heavy beams. However, other rooms seen in passing were more modern in decor and style. Do request a room facing the river - it would be a shame not to take advantage of the mill's serene setting. While the rooms are relatively inexpensive in price the restaurant is expensive.

ALTE RHEINMUHLE
Owner: Othmar Ernst
Junkerstrasse 93
7701 Busingen, Germany
Tel: (07734) 6076 telex: 793788
16 Rooms
Sgl from 75 DM Dbl to 95 DM
Open: All year
Credit Cards: AX, DC
Old mill on the Rhine
Located on the Swiss border

Cochem hugs the banks of the winding River Moselle.   It is a delightful village that thrives on the production of wine and the influx of tourists who come to wander through its streets lined by old houses and to climb to the castle that guards the heights.   Leaning against the remnants of the old town wall, the Alte Thorschenke is a lovely old-fashioned German inn.   From the tiny lobby, a creaking wooden staircase spirals up to the old-fashioned bedchambers.   Several have romantic old four-poster beds and French armoirs.   Request one of these older rooms as the majority of the hotel's accommodations are "dated-modern" rooms built at the rear of the hotel.   Plaid curtains accent the hunting lodge-style dining room with its old-fashioned lamps and high beamed ceiling. Surrounding the village, steep vineyards produce excellent white wines, for Cochem is at the heart of the Moselle wine region.   Consequently wine sampling from the hotel's long wine list or in one of the taverns along the river is a popular pastime.

ALTE THORSCHENKE
Bruckenstrasse 3
5590 Cochem, Germany
Tel: (02671) 7059
51 Rooms
Sgl 70 DM Dbl 160 DM
Open: March 10 to January 3
Credit Cards: All major
Moselle wine village
On the Moselle river
Located 180 km NW of Frankfurt

Miraculously, Cologne's cathedral was not flattened by the Allied bombers that devastated the rest of the city during the Second World War. Its tall, delicate spires still rise above the skyline and the pedestrian square surrounding the cathedral is still the meeting point for visitors from all over the world. Jutting out into the square is the Dom Hotel, one of the grand old stylish hotels of Europe. The public rooms are gracious and formal. The restaurant is a particularly splendid affair, with gleaming paneled walls hung with grand formal portraits where patrons are served by dignified waiters. In summer the terrace cafe provides a less formal dining spot: from here you can almost touch the cathedral - a perfect spot for watching busy Cologne surge by. Heavy marble stairways lead to long bare halls and give no hint of the exquisite, luxurious bedrooms. The bedchambers I saw were grand, high-ceilinged rooms, their large windows hung with beautiful full length drapes, their furniture elegant antiques. Just a word of warning: the rooms are not soundproofed and while the noise of the square recedes late at night, the cathedral bells continue to ring.

DOM HOTEL
Domkloster 2A
5000 Cologne, Germany
Tel: (0221) 233751 telex: 8882919
126 Rooms
Sgl from 260 DM Dbl to 445 DM
(Breakfast not included)
Open: All year
Credit Cards: All major
U.S. Rep: Trust House Forte
Rep. tel: 800-225-5843
Large deluxe hotel
Located next to the cathedral

The Haus Lyskirchen is an excellent choice for a moderately priced hotel in Cologne. The hotel occupies a quiet side street just off the River Rhine. From the pier, only a short distance from the hotel, steamers depart for the popular Rhine river day trip from Cologne to Mainz. A ten-minute stroll through the old town brings you to the cathedral, just far enough away that you can hear the distant echo of its bells. The Haus Lyskirchen is a blend of two sharply contrasting styles: tailored modern and old-fashioned country. To the left of the modern lobby is a small country-style dining room where, if you are too tired to venture out after a busy day's sightseeing, you can enjoy an intimate dinner. Next door an appealing little paneled bar provides a cozy spot for after-dinner drinks. In sharp contrast, a display of modern art leads you to the stark modern breakfast room where you enjoy a sumptuous buffet style breakfast. Bedrooms are either just like a mountain chalet (all in pine and cozy) or modern with elegant mahogany furnishings. A large indoor swimming pool and underground parking are added bonuses. Cologne hosts conventions during January, February, March, April, September and October: if you plan to visit during these times, book well in advance.

HAUS LYSKIRCHEN
Owner: Family Marzorati
Filzengraben 26-32
5000 Cologne, Germany
Tel: (0221) 234891 telex: 8885449
95 Rooms
Sgl from 105 DM Dbl to 210 DM
Credit Cards: All major
Indoor swimming pool
Located 10-minute walk to city center

"Die Deutsche Weinstrasse" means "German Wine Road" and is written on the signposts leading through a string of unpretentious wine-producing villages set amidst the vineyards of the Palatinate.   Ambling from village to village, with stops for wine tasting at taverns and open-to-visit vineyards, is great fun. A most appropriate base for such pursuits is a charming country inn, the Deidesheimer Hof owned by the Hahn Wine family.   Occupying a corner of the village square, the hotel has a formal appearance, for this was once a Bishop's residence.   The inside is all country warmth and good cheer.   The informal dining room - my favorite room - is hung with gay garlands of bread sculptures and wine jugs; the furniture is rustic pine and the food simple and delicious. As you might expect, there are many cozy spots where you can sit and consume wine - the cavernous cellar, the dark beamed bar or, better still, the flower decked terrace that spills into the cobblestoned square in front of the hotel.   The bedrooms come in all shapes and sizes; most are furnished in a very pleasing country modern decor.   Deidesheim's wine festival takes place during the second week of August.

HOTEL DEIDESHEIMER HOF
Owner: Family Hahn
6705 Deidesheim, Germany
Tel: (06326) 1811 or 1812 telex: 454804
26 Rooms
Sgl from 125 DM Dbl to 180 DM
Closed: for Christmas
Credit Cards: All major
U.S. Rep: Romantik Hotels
Rep. tel: 800-826-0015
On the German wine road
Located 120 km SW of Frankfurt

The Hotel Deutsches Haus is a very atmospheric hotel dating from 1440. Its half-timbered facade features ornate wood carving and windowboxes full of vari-colored geraniums. Enter through the old arched doorway into the small, but elegant, lobby and bar area where an old grandfather clock watches over the patrons at the dark wood bar. A graceful wooden staircase leads upstairs to a veritable museum of tapestries, Oriental rugs and antiques lovingly displayed in the hallways. Only 15 bedrooms are offered for overnight guests, and each is unique. Some have pretty flowered porcelain in the bathrooms, and most are furnished with antiques or reproductions. Beamed ceilings and half-timbered walls add character and a sense of history. Downstairs, the traditional restaurant is a favorite with local residents and guests alike who come to enjoy its historic atmosphere and international cuisine. German wines are featured, and the cozy restaurant with its beamed and painted ceiling, arched alcoves and pretty pink tablecloths also doubles as an inviting place to winetaste. It is also astounding to realize that patrons have been tasting wine here for over 400 years, as the town chronicles list the Deutsches Haus as an inn and tavern since 1575.

HOTEL DEUTSCHES HAUS
Owner: Herr Kellerbauer
Weinmarkt 3
8804 Dinkelsbuhl, Germany
Tel: (09851) 2346
15 Rooms
Sgl from 110 DM Dbl to 150 DM
Open: All year
Credit Cards: All major
Walled town on the Romantic Road
Located 120 km NE of Stuttgart

Dinkelsbuhl is a medieval walled town, just as picturesque as, but less crowded than, its more famous neighbor, Rothenburg ob der Tauber. Found on a quiet side street, the Gasthof Zum Goldenen Anker offers outstanding hospitality and dining. Frau and Herr Scharff are the generous hosts who have owned the Gasthof for 20 years. Their son, a well-known chef, has created the gourmet menu served in the three intimate dining rooms. Fine food and wine are served in rustically elegant surroundings of carved pine, lace tablecloths and fresh flowers. Romantic alcoves are perfect for a special occasion, or simply a meal with friends. The low, beamed ceilings are from the original house which was built in 1687. We can attest to the quality and selection of wines, as we were lucky enough to be escorted on a tour of the Goldenen Anker's well-stocked wine cellar, followed by, of course, a winetasting. A restaurant with rooms more than a hotel, the Gasthof Zum Goldenen Anker offers 15 very comfortable guest bedrooms. They are recently refurbished and very fresh, featuring contemporary pine furniture, pretty coverlets and lace curtains. All have a private bath, phone and television with cable channels in English, French and German. Some antique pieces and old paintings add character to the narrow hallways and stairwells.

GASTHOF ZUM GOLDENEN ANKER
Owner: Elfriede Scharff
8804 Dinkelsbuhl, Germany
Tel: (09851) 822
15 Rooms
Sgl from 55 DM Dbl to 85 DM
Open: All year
Credit Cards: All major
Walled town on the Romantic Road
Located 120 km NE of Stuttgart

Hotel Descriptions   151

Although part of the castle itself, the Schloss Hotel Egg sits in a wing curved round a central, walled courtyard and decorative pool under the shadow of dominating turrets and towers. The hotel offers 16 rooms for overnight guests and a fine restaurant that specializes in regional cuisine. Indoors, armor, shields, swords and heavy stone walls set a stage and mood for dining. On a warm afternoon or evening enjoy the tables set round the small pool on a shaded patio. The bed-rooms, found up a steep narrow staircase (a bit difficult to navigate and not very well lit), are very basic but comfortable in their furnishings. My room, a double with bath (number five), was set under the beams and looked out through two low, woodpaned windows onto the surrounding countryside. A loft provided a living room arrangement, an additional small room with a twin bed and spacious bathroom. Not all the rooms are with private bath or w.c. The setting is very tranquil and although I learned in the morning that there were other guests, I heard not a one. There is a definite advantage to sleeping behind thick walls that date back hundreds of years. This is not a first class hotel: it is basic but clean and comfortable, and service with a smile makes up for all that the hotel lacks in modern amenities.

SCHLOSS HOTEL EGG
Owner: Georg L. Hartl
8351 Egg bei Deggendorf, Germany
Tel: (09905) 289
16 Rooms
Dbl from 150 DM to 180 DM
Swimming pool
Located 145 km NE of Munich

Four generations of the Lorentz family have perfected a welcome and capitalized on quality and tradition that is ever present in their hotel. Referenced in local records as early as 1369, the Post now offers extremely modern comforts and facilities. The inn has a number of intimate rooms that serve as restaurants. The main restaurant is very elegant with heavy beams and handpainted scenes that stage an attractive atmosphere. Downstairs is a spectacular bar grill: overlooking the pool through stone arched windows, tapestry covered high back chairs are set around a large open fireplace used to grill steaks and cutlets. Also indoors the adjoining swimming pool resembles a Roman bath house. The Greifen Post has 35 rooms which can be grouped by decor: the "Biedermeyer Zimmers", the "Himmelbett Zimmers" - or four-poster bedrooms, and those with no particular theme but also decorated with stunning reproduction antiques. Finally, there are still a few clean but conventional rooms, that will as time and money afford be renovated. Requests for specific rooms are encouraged and every effort will be made to secure the accommodation of a guest's choice and preference.

ROMANTIK HOTEL GREIFEN POST
Owner: Edward Lorentz
Marktplatz 8
8805 Feuchtwangen, Germany
Tel: (09852) 2004 telex: 61137
35 Rooms
Sgl from 103 DM Dbl to 200 DM
Open: All year
Credit Cards: All major
Swimming pool
Located 170 km NW of Munich

On the outskirts of Frankfurt, conveniently located about fifteen minutes from Frankfurt's popular international airport, is the very polished, sophisticated, well-run Hotel Gravenbruch-Kempinski. Although much larger than most hotels included in this guide, the hotel has so much to offer that we decided to include it. Most of the hotel is new, but the nucleus is old. The architects have constructed the additions to this inn very cleverly, mindful of its origins, combining the best of modern conveniences with olde worlde ambiance. The hotel has a resort atmosphere with various dining rooms, enormous lobbies and a swimming pool. Another plus, the Gravenbruch-Kempinski is set in a forest with excellent paths for strolling or jogging. After a long airline journey, it is quite refreshing to take a walk in the woods before a bite to eat and going to bed. You will find yourself refreshed the next day and ready to "hit the road".

HOTEL GRAVENBRUCH-KEMPINSKI
Owner: Kempinski AG
Manager: Gunther Haug
Neu-Isenburg 2
6078 Frankfurt, Germany
Tel: (06102) 5050 telex: 417673
317 Rooms
Sgl from 338 DM Dbl to 431 DM
Open: All year
Credit Cards: All major
U.S. Rep: Leading Hotels of the World
Rep. tel: 800-223-6800
Tennis, swimming pool
Located on Rte 459, 11 km SE of Frankfurt

Our visit to the Schloss Hotel Kronberg coincided with that of visiting delegates and bedrooms were closed off for security reasons. However, based on the few rooms I saw and the sumptuous sophistication of the public rooms, I feel comfortable in recommending the Schloss Kronberg as an excellent choice for a hotel. Northwest of Frankfurt, a convenient half an hour drive by the autoroute from the Frankfurt airport, this was once a gathering place for European royalty and most of the ruling monarchs were at one time guests here. The hotel has a number of grand halls impressive with their high ceilings and adorning tapestries. Coffee is often served in the stately library in front of its large stone fireplace, and the adjoining Blue Parlor room is frequently reserved for private functions and luncheons. At the end of the hall a beautiful wood paneled dining room achieves intimacy and grandeur in its decor. The Schloss Kronberg was built originally in 1888 as a private home, and has been offering rooms to guests for over fifty years. For ten years prior to that it served as a casino for the American military.

SCHLOSS HOTEL KRONBERG
Manager: G. Kohler
Hainstrasse 25
6242 Kronberg in Taunus, Germany
Tel: (06173) 70101 telex: 415424
59 Rooms
Sgl from 220 DM Dbl to 365 DM
Credit Cards: AX, DC
Open: All year
Golf
Located 17 km NW of Frankfurt

How fortunate that driving rain drove us into Oberkirch's Weinstuben for a fortifying drink, for we discovered that it is also a darling inn. Oberkirch's Weinstuben is actually located in two buildings. The principal building sits on Munsterplatz in the shadow of Freiburg's striking cathedral, the other just a short cobblestone block away. The Weinstuben serves a very satisfying lunch or dinner in a very congenial and cozy atmosphere. Beamed ceilings, wooden tables, white linen and contented chatter set the mood for the cozy restaurant. It is a popular place to dine for anyone familiar with Freiburg and understandably so. The 31 rooms are found either directly above the weinstube or in the neighboring building, are all comfortable and very attractive in a traditional decor. The hallways are well maintained, quiet and enhanced by lovely prints. It is somewhat difficult to maneuver by auto through the pedestrian district but the hotel provides a map and directions for parking. Again, as a result of spending time in the weinstube I learned from another patron that the senior Frau Oberkirch died in 1985 but it was her dream to restore the cathedral and she invested quite a sum of money to pursue it. It was touching but bittersweet to see that restorations are currently being carried out.

OBERKIRCH'S WEINSTUBEN
Owner: Family Johner-Oberkirch
Munsterplatz 13
7800 Freiburg im Breisgau, Germany
Tel: (0761) 31011
31 Rooms
Sgl from 61 DM Dbl to 189 DM
Closed: December 22 to January 20
Wonderful old town in Black Forest
Located 295 km S of Frankfurt

The Waldhotel Friedrichsruhe, a complex of buildings set on spacious grounds in a very idyllic and rural setting, is run along the lines of a deluxe hotel as opposed to an inn, with an impersonal, formal reception. Managed for ten years by Herr Eiermann, the Waldhotel Friedrichsruhe provides deluxe room accommodations, excellent dining, facilities for sportsmen and a peaceful environment. The main dining room is very elegant: walls covered in rust colored material to match the floor-to-ceiling drapes, gilded chandeliers, and tables set with white linen and dramatic fresh flower arrangements. The breakfast room, by contrast, is very simple and opens onto the lush green gardens. The Hunters Restaurant is a charming gathering spot, more country in decor, with wood backed chairs and green print fabrics. The bedrooms, ranging in decor from traditional to modern, are found in various buildings on the property. Set in a rotunda and exposed to the garden through floor to ceiling windows are a lovely indoor - outdoor swimming pool and a sauna.

WALDHOTEL FRIEDRICHSRUHE
Manager: Lothar Eiermann
7111 Friedrichsruhe, Germany
Tel: (07941) 7078 telex: 74498
41 Rooms
Sgl from 170 DM Dbl to 478 DM
Closed: last two weeks of January
Credit Cards: All major
U.S. Rep: David Mitchell
Rep. tel: 800-372-1323
Swimming pool, golf, tennis
Located 97 km NE of Stuttgart

There is something very endearing about the simplicity of the Schloss Fursteneck. One would never just happen upon this hotel. It is set in the Bavarian Hills in a village that is mostly comprised of a castle and a church. By no means luxurious, this hotel, however, sparkles under the management of Erika Vilhelm. She bustles about with a warm smile and pride that keep the twelve rooms under her care spotless. Erika sees that the menu highlights the regional specialties and that her garden and windowboxes are full of blooms and color. Under arched ceilings, the restaurant is very cozy; tables are decked with either blue or red checked cloths. There are actually three adjoining dining rooms to choose from: the Gaststube, the Jagerzimmer (a round room with a hunting motif that overlooks a steep drop to the River Ohr), and the Kaminzimmer (named for the fireplace that warms it). The hotel has only two rooms with full bath and private toilet. Again, I stress the rooms are simple but sweet with matching prints used for the comforter covers and the curtains. In this region one can hike between hotels. Set out with only a luncheon pack and have your bags delivered to your next hotel. Contact Erika for specific details and arrangements.

SCHLOSS FURSTENECK
Owner: Adrian Forster
Manager: Erika Vilhelm
8397 Fursteneck, Germany
Tel: (08505) 1473
12 Rooms
25 DM per person per night
Open: All year
Credit Cards: All major
Located 195 km NE of Munich

Set under the shadow of Germany's highest peak, the Zugspitze, Clausing's Posthotel affords a convenient, but somewhat noisy, location on one of the main streets in the town of Garmisch. Just steps away from elegant boutiques and ski slopes, this small hotel, once a postal station, has been managed by the Clausing family for five generations. Members of the family can be seen welcoming guests in the reception area, or assisting with a selection from the menu in one of their fine restaurants. Families might prefer the cafe-style Klause; oompah music tempts one into the popular Post Hornd'l; unobstructed views of the Zugspitze and town's street activity are the reason that many settle at the Terrace, and the Stuberl prides itself on atmosphere and fine cuisine. The bedrooms are large, spacious and well appointed. Although rooms at the front of the hotel enjoy breathtaking views of the Zugspitze, I would strongly advise requesting a room at the back to avoid the constant sound of traffic.

CLAUSING'S POSTHOTEL
Owner: Family Clausing
Marienplatz 12
8100 Garmisch-Partenkirchen, Germany
Tel: (08821) 7090 Fax: (08821) 709205
35 Rooms
Sgl from 132 DM Dbl to 253 DM
Open: All year
Credit Cards: All major
U.S. Rep: Romantik Hotels
Rep. tel: 800-826-0015
Located 89 km S of Munich

Located in the historic section of Partenkirchen, the Gasthof Fraundorfer has been in the Fraundorfer family for 80 years and is still very much a homey, family-run inn. Its facade is decorated with murals and windowboxes of healthy red geraniums, while inside a marvelously atmospheric restaurant awaits. Walls and ceilings entirely in mellow knotty pine foster a warm, rustic feeling here, where tradition is taken seriously. Frau Fraundorfer explained that one of the wooden tables in the room is what is called in German a "stammtisch". This table is the exclusive territory of a specific group of regulars, and each person in the group has his own place at which he always sits. In fact, some of the chairs have brass plaques engraved with the occupant's name. Photos of "stammtisch" regulars adorn the wall above the table, some dating back 50 years. Home-cooked meals accompanied by German beers and wines are served in this charming dining room. A worn staircase leads to the guest bedrooms which vary in size and furnishings, although most are in a reproduction Bavarian style. Do not expect elegance, but homey comfort. Most rooms have private bath, and some have phones, televisions, and balconies. This inn is truly a friendly place, where family photographs of the healthy, blond Fraundorfers decorate the upstairs hallway and Bavarian music is performed every week.

GASTHOF FRAUNDORFER
Owner: Family Fraundorfer
8100 Garmisch-Partenkirchen, Germany
Tel: (08821) 2176
24 Rooms
Sgl from 38 DM Dbl to 130 DM
Closed: Nov 15 to Dec 15 & 3 weeks in Apr
Credit Cards: AX, VS
Restaurant
Located 89 km S of Munich

To meet the demands of the 1936 Olympics, the two villages of Partenkirchen and Garmisch merged. The distinction between what were once two towns is still very apparent today and Partenkirchen seems to have preserved most of the charm. On a colorful old street, opposite the church, the Posthotel Partenkirchen reflects its past history as a post station. Four generations of the Stahl family have maintained the olde worlde tradition and standard of service. Handsome antiques are still displayed in all the public rooms and maids are always busy polishing and scrubbing each and every corner. A cozy bar sits just off the grand entry and is warmed by a lovely oven. Trunks and painted armoirs line the hallways that lead to delightful accommodations. Rather than a particular one or two, it seemed that the majority of the hotel's 60 rooms were decorated with cherished antiques and lovely prints and fabrics. On the first floor, the largest room is number 2. Wood paneled, it looks out over the back streets through thick walls. Although smaller, number 53, paneled from floor to ceiling in rich wood, is completely surrounded by a balcony, and enjoys an unobstructed view of the Zugspitze.

POSTHOTEL PARTENKIRCHEN
Owner: Otto & Lisa Stahl
Ludwigstrasse 49
8100 Garmisch-Partenkirchen, Germany
Tel: (08821) 51067 telex: 59611
60 Rooms
Sgl from 89 Dbl to 202 DM
Open: All year
Credit Cards: All major
Lovely traditional hotel
Located 89 km S of Munich

Often I have included a town because of a wonderful hotel but in this case I am including a hotel because of a wonderful town. Made rich by mining in the nearby Harz Mountains, Goslar was a flourishing regional capital before Columbus set sail for America. Time has been kind, and wandering the narrow cobbled streets is like taking a walk into a history book. Occupying a corner of the large pedestrian market square, the Kaiserworth was built in 1494 as the guild house of the cloth-workers. The impressive facade, with carvings of emperors beneath the eaves, was completed in the 17th century. Inside, the public rooms do not quite live up to the promise of the splendid exterior - the decor in the vaulted dining room and paneled breakfast room was a little worn at the time of my visit. Up the grand curving staircase the bedrooms are all decorated in the same decor, with fresh white walls and old-style dark wood furniture accented by maroon and white drapes and bed ruffles. The rooms at the front of the hotel are large and spacious; those at the rear are smaller. Step outside your hotel at six in the evening and watch the concert of the city clock whose four different scenes represent the thousand year-old mining history of the region.

HOTEL KAISERWORTH
Manager: Udo Mehrenes
Markt 3
3380 Goslar, Germany
Tel: (05321) 21111 telex: 953874
55 Rooms
Sgl from 65 DM Dbl to 180 DM
Open: All year
Credit Cards: All major
Wonderful old town
Located 250 km S of Hamburg

A curved, dark wooden staircase leads to the second floor of the Schloss Hotel Grunwald, where the atmosphere is more like a museum that takes in guests than a hotel. Each room has very high ceilings and is uniquely furnished in priceless antiques. The hallways are also filled with old paintings, carved wooden statues, and large antique pieces. The third floor is the former maids' quarters, thus the ceilings are lower and rooms smaller in their dimensions. Rooms are not as lavishly furnished, although all have antique touches and are very tasteful and refined. The hotel's beautiful setting high on a hillside overlooking the Isar river affords gorgeous views from the pleasant outdoor terrace, where guests can sit under the chestnut trees and enjoy an open air lunch or perhaps a before dinner cocktail. Inside, the ambiance of the dark wood paneled restaurant is more that of a Bavarian hunting lodge than of an elegant museum as in the upstairs rooms. Warm rose tablecloths complement pretty dried flower arrangements, gleaming silver, china, and glassware. Traditional regional cuisine is served here as well as a fresh, "nouvelle" style of cooking. Great arched windows frame the breathtaking view over the terrace to the forested hills and down to the Isar River. Relax in this inviting restaurant and enjoy a delicious meal without fear of the bill, as the menu is very reasonably priced.

SCHLOSS HOTEL GRUNWALD
Owner: Florian Voigt
8022 Grunwald, Germany
Tel: (089) 641935 telex: 5218 817
16 Rooms
Sgl from 105 DM Dbl to 230 DM
Closed: January 1 to 15
Credit Cards: All major
Parking, terrace
Located 10 km from the center of Munich

The old saying, "don't judge a book by its cover", certainly applies to the Hotel-Restaurant Adler. This recently built hotel-restaurant is set back from the road and partly hidden by trees, thus not too much character is evident from the exterior. However, the moment one enters the foyer with its old baby carriage filled with plants and flowers, it is obvious that a treat is in store. The warm open lobby area has a dark tiled floor, comfortable couches, and dried flower arrangements which all combine for a real feeling of old Germany. The Boddicker family has owned and managed the Hotel-Restaurant Adler since 1971 with obvious care and pride. They have decorated the restaurant and breakfast room with cherished family antiques and achieved the ideal balance of country elegance and "gemutlichkeit". The focal point of the charming breakfast room is a large, 100-year-old organ, now converted to a player piano which plays traditional "oom-pah-pah" tunes. The main restaurant offers a delicious menu including tempting pastries and desserts which are a house specialty. Each table is a cozy corner unto itself, adorned with white tablecloths, fresh flowers, china and glassware. The 15 bedrooms are all very comfortable and tastefully decorated; most with some antique accents. All have private bath. The Hotel-Restaurant Adler promises a gourmet meal and a good night's rest; German country inn style.

HOTEL-RESTAURANT ADLER
Owner: Family R. Boddicker
7809 Gutach/Breisgau, Germany
Tel: (07681) 7022
15 Rooms
Sgl from 50 DM Dbl to 100 DM
Closed: January
Credit Cards: AX, DC, MC
Located 20 km NE of Freiberg

Hamburg is the hub of northern Germany. Far more than an important seaport and business center, it is a city of great beauty offering a rich and varied social and cultural menu. Just north of the city center you find Alster Lake: with this expanse of water at its front and a tranquil garden at its rear, the Hotel Prem occupies a handsome downtown Hamburg location. What were originally two large townhouses were converted into a small hotel by Mr and Mrs Prem more than 75 years ago. The downstairs is small: a lounge area leads to a bar and beyond an airy restaurant overlooks the garden. The restaurant, decorated in shades of beige and white and with arrangements of fresh flowers, brightens even the gloomiest Hamburg day. In summer the pretty garden is set with tables and chairs for outside dining. Accented with fine antiques, the bedrooms retain their high ceilings which give a spacious feeling. A few lovely rooms have retained their original ornate plasterwork ceilings. The staff speak excellent English and really care that you enjoy your holiday. Hamburg's sightseeing attractions are quite a long walk away, but only steps from your front door are the walking paths that encircle the lake. As an added bonus, the hotel provides discounted rates for guests staying on weekends.

HOTEL PREM
Manager: Iutta Breyer
An der Alster 9
2000 Hamburg, Germany
Tel: (04024) 5454 telex: 2163115
49 Rooms
Sgl from 136 DM Dbl to 273 DM
Open: All year
Credit Cards: All major
Located just N of city center

One fortunate day while exploring the Black Forest region, we stumbled across the picturesque village of Haslach.   This little town is centrally located in the middle of the Black Forest area, and as we searched for an atmospheric restaurant for lunch, we happily spotted the Hotel Gasthof Zum Raben.   Its pretty half-timbered facade features a small turret flanked by balconies, and windowboxes overflowing with pretty red geraniums.   The Zum Raben is located just off Haslach's historic market square, and is the town's oldest inn.   Only German is spoken here, but the welcome is warm and genuine.   Enter through the cozy restaurant, where a reasonably priced, traditional menu is served.   The dark wood paneled room with its old parquet floor is brightened by fresh wild flower bouquets.   An old green tile fireplace, old paintings and pretty cushions on the wooden chairs complete this historic and homey picture, a true "Schwarzwald slice of life".   A back staircase leads to the small bedrooms, most of which share a bath.   Some have antique painted furniture, but, in general, the rooms and hallways are very modest.   The Hotel Gasthof Zum Raben is a bargain for those travelers who seek "local color" and do not mind simple accommodation.

GASTHOF ZUM RABEN
Owner: Gunter Fackler
Kinzigtal
7612 Haslach, Germany
Tel: (07832) 2270
10 Rooms
Sgl from 27 DM Dbl to 52 DM
Closed: first 2 weeks in November
Credit Cards: None
Black Forest village
Located 35 km NE of Freiburg

The 300-year-old Zur Backmulde enjoys a quiet location off the pedestrian street of Heidelberg's picturesque "old town". It is a very small and atmospheric establishment which offers an intimate restaurant of twelve tables, and seven bedrooms for guests.   Pass under the old stone arched doorway to enter the softly lit restaurant filled with fresh flowers, antique pieces, knickknacks, and even a "kitchen witch".   An old cradle holds a display of dried flowers, harvest breads, and regional wines.   One is tempted to hide away and spend the entire afternoon in this cozy nook, the only reminder of the world outside coming from the stained lead glass windows letting in the sun's rays.   There is no lack of good food, as the menu here is extensive and changes daily.   Frau Klose provides a solicitous welcome to guests staying overnight in her homey bedrooms, all of which have a shower and w.c.   Lovely antiques dress up the hallways and several of the bedrooms, while fresh and dried flower bouquets brighten the atmosphere throughout.   The breakfast room is very unusual and features a small fountain under a central skylight, surrounded by an abundance of green plants.   The room is decorated in forest green tones and gives the feeling of an oasis.   Certainly a tranquil way to begin the day, with the soothing background noise of the fountain's running water.

ZUR BACKMULDE
Owner: Family Klose
Schiffgasse 11
6900 Heidelberg, Germany
Tel: (06221) 22551
7 Rooms
Sgl from 85 DM Dbl to 105 DM
Closed: January 15 to February 15
Credit Cards: None
Located in the old town of Heidelberg

The Hotel Garni am Kornmarkt is located in Old Heidelberg near the Tourist Office and beginning of the pedestrian section of the Hauptstrasse. It is tranquilly located on a pretty little square which is very near the Heidelberg Castle tram station. This informal little bed and breakfast hotel offers the best of homey hospitality, location, and price. The pretty facade is painted a dusky red with white trim. A former private home, the house is 250 years old. Walk past bikes propped up in the hall to the tiny reception area where Ingeborg Wachter will extend her warm welcome. She offers 16 guest bedrooms, half of which have private bath. Clean, modern furnishings make for comfortable, if unimaginative, accommodation. Room size varies, and some have views of the famous Heidelberg Castle on the hill above. Breakfast is served in a very inviting room furnished in old tapestry chairs and tables and a large antique sideboard. Bright yellow daisies adorn the tables as Frau Wachter serves a satisfying Continental breakfast. Her parakeets chirp in the next room as guests chat and make sightseeing plans for the day. This is an easy task from the Hotel Garni am Kornmarkt, as the atmospheric old section of Heidelberg is literally at the front door, and most sights are within easy walking distance.

HOTEL GARNI AM KORNMARKT
Owner: Frau Ingeborg Wachter
Kornmarkt 7
6900 Heidelberg, Germany
Tel: (06221) 24325
16 Rooms
Sgl from 50 DM Dbl to 120 DM
Closed: December 24 to January 15
Credit Cards: AX
Parking garage nearby
Located centrally in the old town of Heidelberg

A warm and gracious welcome is assured at the charming Hotel Reichspost in Heidelberg. The hotel is quiet, located on a peaceful residential street slightly removed from the historic section of town. The pretty yellow facade and white shutters are freshly painted, and complemented by geraniums in the ground floor windowboxes. Inside the small entryhall guests are greeted by hosts Herr and Frau Obrecht. The hotel business is in the Obrechts' blood, for they have been hoteliers all their lives, as was Herr Obrecht's father before him. A large oil painting of "Grandfather Obrecht" hangs in the front hall, as well as an engraving of the grand Hotel Strand which he built. Other prints and paintings in the hallways and up the winding staircase depict all kinds of sailboats, since the Obrecht family's second passion after hotelkeeping is sailing. It seems they take a month off every year and disappear for an extended cruise on their own sailboat. Of the 30 guest bedrooms, half have private baths. Character is added to the bedrooms and hallways by family antiques and Oriental rugs. The breakfast room and lounge is decorated in yellow and white with lace tablecloths and fresh flowers on small round tables. The effect is cheerful and pretty, a welcoming place to begin the day.

HOTEL REICHSPOST
Owner: Family Obrecht
Gaisbergstrasse 38
6900 Heidelberg, Germany
Tel: (06221) 22252
30 Rooms
Sgl from 90 DM Dbl to 110 DM
Closed: January and February
Credit Cards: None
Elevator
Located six blocks west of the train station in Heidelberg

Heidelberg is a romantic, beguiling old university town with one main street, the Hauptstrasse, that captures most of the atmosphere. It is here that you will find the Hotel Zum Ritter, afforded one of the best locations in town. From its rooftop garden you will have an incomparable view of the old city. Owned by the Kuchelmeisters, the Zum Ritter is managed as a very professional and first class city hotel. The majority of the accommodations are comfortable, but sterile and modern in decor. The hotel serves a nice standard breakfast that is included in the price of the room and at night the restaurant is lit with candles and takes on a very intimate and romantic atmosphere. The public areas are decorated with antiques and the hotel's stately facade dates from 1592 when the master builder, Carolus Belier, imprinted the gold sign still hanging above the door. Official records show the building served as a town hall for a decade before it became the Hotel Zum Ritter. If driving, follow signs to Parkplatz 12. From there it is only a few blocks to the hotel.

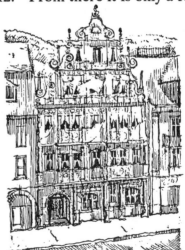

HOTEL ZUM RITTER
Owner: Georg Kuchelmeister
Manager: H.J. Gerber
Hauptstrasse 178
6900 Heidelberg, Germany
Tel: (06221) 20203 telex: 461506
34 Rooms
Sgl from 115 DM Dbl to 260 DM
Open: All year
Credit Cards: All major
U.S. Rep: Romantik Hotels
Rep. tel: 800-826-0015
Parking garage nearby
Located 80 km S of Frankfurt

This posthotel carries the name of the family who has owned it since 1863. Monch's Posthotel exudes elegance and olde worlde charm as opposed to the flavor of a simple country inn.   The family is still involved in the management but you will be greeted by very gracious and efficient girls, all dressed in colorful dirndls. Through a small arched wooden doorway is a delightful a la carte restaurant, nestled in the oldest part of the building.   Here lunch, tea and dinner are served either in dark wooden booths or at the individual tables.   Grey-blue linens blend beautifully with blue tiles, and freshly pressed white curtains adorn the windows. Off the entry is a larger, more formal dining room.   With a high ceiling and dressed in soft yellow, the room is very airy and overlooks the garden through full length windows.   In summer breakfast is enjoyed in the garden.   The bedrooms all differ but are consistent in style and attractive decor, decorated in soft colors, patterned wallpapers and traditional furnishings.   Bathrooms are sparkling clean and modern.   The hotel also has a lovely outdoor swimming pool in a delightful garden setting.

MONCH'S POSTHOTEL
Owner: Family Monch
Doblerstrasse 2
7506 Bad Herrenalb, Germany
Tel: (07083) 2002 telex: 7245123
50 Rooms 9 Apts
Sgl from 113 DM Dbl to 279 DM
Open: All year
Credit Cards: AX, DC
Swimming pool
Located 170 km S of Frankfurt

Bad Hersfeld is a handsome North German town. At its heart lies a large market square lined with old burghers' houses, part of which has been turned into a pedestrian mall. It is in this pedestrian zone, with its tables and chairs spilling over onto the square, that you find the Hotel Zum Stern. Bustling and welcoming, the inn has been offering hospitality to weary travelers for over 500 years. In recent years, as the volume of trade has grown, the hotel has expanded back from the square so that accommodations are provided in an old section and a modern extension. An indoor swimming pool is found at the rear of the building overlooking the garden. Try to secure one of the darling rooms in the original hostelry. With their blackened beams, creaking floorboards and antique furniture, they are a real prize. Regional specialties highlight the extensive menu. What is special here is the kindness and hospitality of the Kniese family who have owned this inn for four generations.

HOTEL ZUM STERN
Owner: Family Kniese
Linggplatz 11
6430 Bad Hersfeld, Germany
Tel: (06621) 72007
49 Rooms
Sgl from 82 DM Dbl to 169 DM
Open: All year
Credit Cards: All major
U.S. Rep: Romantik Hotels
Rep. tel: 800-226-0015
Swimming pool
Located 170 km NE of Frankfurt

The Park Hotel Adler is truly a very elegant and luxurious hotel. Its facilities and service will guarantee any guest a comfortable and memorable stay. The Adler has 74 rooms and suites and yet the Riesterer family has managed the hotel for generations with the personal touch of a country inn. A pale yellow building trimmed with green shutters and flower boxes, the Adler sits on many acres of its own private park, with intriguing footpaths to follow. The extensive facilities include a sauna, pool, jacuzzi, massage, bowling and tennis. There is a small fee for use of all but the pool and jacuzzi. Hinterzarten is a favorite year-round resort for sports enthusiasts who hike the surrounding footpaths, ride, fish, ski, skate and toboggan. Although more formal than an inn, the standard of service and refined quality of the Adler as a hotel make it impossible not to include it in this guide.

PARK HOTEL ADLER
Owner: Family Riesterer
Adlerplatz 3
7824 Hinterzarten, Germany
Tel: (07652) 711 telex: 772692
74 Rooms
Sgl from 152 DM Dbl to 456 DM
Open: All year
Credit Cards: All major
U.S. Rep: Leading Hotels of the World
Rep. tel: 800-223-6800
Swimming pool, tennis, sauna, bowling
Located 161 km SW of Stuttgart

If your arrival at the Sassenhof is midday you will most likely find Frau Pfeiffer dressed in a starched lace apron, supervising the cleaning and presentation of each of her guest rooms.   An extremely handsome woman, she and her husband strive to achieve an atmosphere of a private home with the advantages of very personalized service.   Richly polished woods and antique furnishings adorn the public rooms and artistic fresh flower arrangements prepared by Frau Pfeiffer add splashes of color everywhere.   The Sassenhof has a gorgeous dining area where breakfast is unfortunately the only formal meal served.   Tea, however, can be enjoyed in the afternoons and each room is thoughtfully provided with freshly pressed linen and dishes.   Drinks and bread are conveniently available upon request, encouraging guests to buy their own meats and cheeses and to prepare their own light suppers or lunches.   The halls that lead to the bedrooms are warmed by soft lighting, handsome prints, red carpet covered in Oriental throw rugs, and heavy wooden doors and doorways.   Each room is individual in its decor but all are tastefully and attractively decorated and arranged by Frau Pfeiffer.   In this small guest house it is surprising to find a very large, attractive swimming pool.

SASSENHOF
Owner: Family Pfeiffer
Alderweg 17
7824 Hinterzarten, Germany
Tel: (07652) 1515
22 Rooms
Sgl from 62 Dbl to 165 DM
Closed: November to mid December
Swimming pool
Located 161 km SW of Stuttgart

The Hotel Gasthof Zum Engel, located high on a hill, is a good sized, typically German country hotel and restaurant. The large building is built in farmhouse style, with a pleasant tree-shaded terrace in front, providing a perfect spot for an open air lunch. The Zum Engel is capably run by the Hagenmeier family and very good English is spoken. The feeling is very welcoming as one enters the long, tiled entry hall with its gilt mirror and fresh flower arrangement in a large copper pitcher. The large, friendly restaurant is located just off this entryhall. It is an airy room with many windows, ladder backed wooden chairs, warm light wood walls, brass chandeliers and fresh flower arrangements. The extensive menu offers a wide variety of choices including game dishes such as pheasant, duck, rabbit and venison. Oriental carpeted stairs lead up to the 28 guest rooms, 21 of which have private bath. The highlight of these rooms is their pretty views of the surrounding rolling green and forested hills of the Black Forest countryside. Guests will find tasteful contemporary furnishings in their spotlessly clean rooms. The Hotel Gasthof Zum Engel is a restful spot to eat a delicious meal and spend a comfortable night while exploring this popular vacation region.

HOTEL GASTHOF ZUM ENGEL
Owner: Family Bertolk Hagenmeier
7801 Horben-Langackern
bei Freiberg im Breisgau, Germany
Tel: (0761) 29111 and 29112
28 Rooms
Sgl from 80 DM Dbl to 120 DM
Open: March to November
Credit Cards: All major
Black Forest village
Located 5 km S of Freiburg

High above the beautiful Moselle Valley is one of those rare, perfect hideaways - the Historische Bergmuhle. It is a little complicated getting to the hotel; a detailed map will certainly aid you in finding the Rhaunen turnoff from the road 327 that runs to the south of the Moselle. You will find the Historische Bergmuhle a short drive from the junction, about half a mile beyond the tiny village of Horbruch. The Historische Bergmuhle was once an old mill. Bedrooms in the old mill are named after country animals and, apart from being beautifully decorated, are stocked with thoughtful little extras that make a stay memorable - proper sewing kits, hair spray and perfume. The four new rooms in the granary are equally as lovely in their country-pretty decor. Rudiger and Anneliese Liller are your charming hosts: their hotel looks so appealing because Anneliese is a creative interior decorator. A little corner room honors Napoleon, for the mill has associations with this famous soldier. The story goes that in 1804 Napoleon sold the mill to raise money and the enterprising new owner had the foresight to realise that once Napoleon had left, the original owner would reclaim his property. To guard against this happening, he had the mill taken apart and erected 25 kilometers away in this quiet green valley outside the village of Horbruch.

HOTEL HISTORISCHE BERGMUHLE
Owner: Family Liller
6541 Horbruch-Hunsruck, Germany
Tel: (06543) 4041
11 Rooms
Sgl from 55 DM Dbl to 180 DM
Closed: mid January to mid February
Credit Cards: All major
Located 130 km W of Frankfurt

Just 30 kilometers from the fascinating city of Wurzburg, the Zehntkeller, Romantik Hotel and wine house, is also convenient to the wine region at the foot of the Schwan mountains. Once a tax collection point for the church, and hence a most unpopular building, the Zehntkeller is now a chosen destination of many. Iphofen is a small quiet village and it is amazing to find the traffic coming and going from the inn: the specialties of the menu attract diners from the outlying regions. The restaurant is actually a number of rooms on the first floor and serviced by gracious girls dressed in attractive dirndls. The hotel rooms found in the main building above the restaurant are all lovely and are well appointed with modern bathrooms. Single rooms are found on the top floor. In an annex that backs onto a walled garden, a new wing of rooms has been added to accommodate guests who want to linger for a stay of more than a few days.

ROMANTIK HOTEL ZEHNTKELLER
Owner: Heinrich Seufert
Bahnhofstrasse 12
8715 Iphofen, Germany
Tel: (09323) 3062
44 Rooms
Sgl from 78 DM Dbl to 160 DM
Closed: last 2 weeks of January
U.S. Rep: Romantik Hotels
Rep. tel: 800-826-0015
Home grown wines
Located 248 km NW of Munich

Under the management of Hartwig Leyk, pride and care are evident in every aspect of the Hotel Zum Goldenen Pflug (translated as the "golden plow").   This gem of a hotel is located in the little farming village of Ising not far from "Mad Ludwig's" dramatic castle on a tiny island in the Chiemsee.   The reception area and spacious inviting bar are found in what were once the cow byres.   The charming dining rooms: Fischer Stube, Gaststube and Jagerstube are in the barn.   Although all three restaurants have a different theme of decor, the food is good and attractively presented in each.   The bedrooms are scattered around the complex and, depending on their location, vary in theme but are all exceptional in comfort and decor.   Accommodations are found in the stables, in the old blacksmith's abode - cozy under beams and country in decor - and some dear rooms are located in a house set all on its own.   Off the reception area is a wing of rooms more recently built but traditional in decor.   Surrounding the hotel is a large estate.   The hotel also offers its own riding stables and trainer for guests on a longer stay who wish to ride.

ZUM GOLDENEN PFLUG
Owner: Konstantin Magalow
Manager: Hartwig Leyk
Kirchberg 3, Ising am Chiemsee
8224 Chieming, Germany
Tel: (08667) 790 telex: 56542
54 Rooms
Sgl from 89 DM Dbl to 145 DM
Open: All year
Credit Cards: AX
On Lake Chiemsee
Located 165 km SE of Munich

The introduction to this marvelous castle hotel is first an expanse of lawn, intricate turrets and then an old timbered courtyard. Up a flight of stairs, the hotel entrance is a majestic banquet hall. The dining room is very regal. Take notice of a handsome, intricately inlaid door, lovely flower arrangements and the crest of the family above both entrances. The present family has lived in the castle as far back as 927. Herr Bircks, both manager and chef, is a charming man, exuding pride in the castle and offering a warm welcome for each guest. The breakfast room looks out through large windows onto the lush surrounding countryside. Climb a steep staircase in the direction of the bedchambers onto a terrace that also enjoys an expansive view and is used in warmer months for dining. Down a timbered hallway, the bedrooms are all named for renowned actors and many overlook either the valley or the weathered tiles of another castle wing. The highlight of the adjoining armaments museum is an iron hand, unique because of its moveable parts. In summer months the courtyard becomes a stage for afternoon and evening plays. Also, to the delight of children and adults, a steam train provides scenic rides through the valley.

BURGHOTEL GOTZENBURG
Owner: Family Von Berlichingen
Manager: J. Bircks
7109 Jagsthausen, Germany
Tel: (07943) 2222
15 Rooms
Sgl from 60 DM Dbl to 100 DM
Closed: November to mid March
Credit Cards: VS, DC, AX
Located 82 km N of Stuttgart

Sylt is beautiful; a narrow island of sand dunes jutting into the North Sea atop Germany's far northern border. Sheltered behind the dunes, the village of Kampen flies the British and German flags in the garden of Hinchley Wood, the home of Sam and Anne Smith. More than 25 years ago, Anne brought her husband and three young children from England to her island home and they turned their house into an English bed and breakfast. Sam's oil paintings crowd the walls around the chintz sofa and chairs which look just as "at home" here as their counterparts do in proper English parlors. . The bedrooms are tiny and neat, about half of them having private bathrooms. When I visited, the house was crowded with German holidaymakers and Anne happily had her guests underfoot as she bustled around making breakfast. Sam entered the dining room to a chorus of "Good Morning", a greeting from his guests. His inquiries as to the weather, their breakfast, and their plans for the day were all in English - for Sam speaks only a few words of German. While Anne cares for their guests, Sam entertains them with his reminiscences of his career in the Royal Air Force and laments the island's lack of interest in his favorite game - cricket. Anne and Sam's special brand of sincere warmth and hospitality attracts visitors from all over the world and from all walks of life.

HINCHLEY WOOD
Owner: Anne & Sam Smith
2285 Kampen-Sylt, Germany
Tel: (04651) 41546
12 Rooms
Sgl from 95 DM Dbl to 130 DM
Open: All year
English style Bed & Breakfast
Located 230 km NW of Hamburg

Sylt, a sand-dune island located in the northernmost tip of Germany, is reached by taking the car-train across the narrow causeway linking the island to the mainland - a 45-minute ride. The Benen Diken Hof is one of the island's loveliest hotels. The hotel is several squat Friesian farmhouses joined into a complex by means of glass corridors that appear to bring the outdoors indoors. Decorated throughout in white and cream with accents of pale pink and blue, the hotel is "decorator perfect", warm and welcoming. After a walk along the sand dunes in the bracing sea air, you return to the hotel to pamper yourself with a sauna and a massage or a relaxing swim. The hotel's greatest asset is its owner, Claas Johannsen. In the evening he can be found, surrounded by his collection of old model fire engines, hosting the hotel's cozy bar. His warmth and graciousness transcend the language barrier and make you feel at home. The restaurant serves only breakfast: but do not worry: the small island abounds with restaurants. A particular recommendation goes to the restaurant Landhaus Stricker in the adjacent village of Tinnum, offering elegant gourmet dining in a Friesian farmhouse.

BENEN DIKEN HOF
Owner: Claas Johannsen
Postlach 20
2280 Keitum-Sylt, Germany
Tel: (04651) 31035
40 Rooms
Sgl from 100 DM Dbl to 300 DM
Open: All year
Credit Cards: All major
U.S. Rep: Romantik Hotels
Rep. tel: 800-826-0015
Located 230 km NW of Hamburg

The Ruhr Valley is the major heavy industry area of Germany. Smokestacks and factories extend for mile after mile, then suddenly end, giving way to pockets of beautiful countryside. In one such green oasis lies the Schloss Hugenpoet, an imposing fortress surrounded by a water-filled moat where large carp swim lazily. There has been a fortification on this site for over one thousand years, and during violent periods of history several castles were destroyed. The present structure has existed since 1650. The interior presents a castle in tiptop condition: the lobby is dominated by an impressive black marble staircase; a grouping of fine furniture stands in front of the huge carved fireplace, while the surrounding walls host a picture gallery of fine oil paintings. This is a grand castle where the bedchambers were given spacious proportions. Many are furnished with fine 16th-century furniture. Downstairs, the dining rooms are baronial in their size, each dominated by a grand carved fireplace. Boasting famous chefs and gourmet cuisine, the dining rooms command a large, loyal, local following while still giving impeccable service to the hotel residents.

SCHLOSS HUGENPOET
Owner: Mr Neumann
4300 Kettwig, Germany
Tel: (02054) 6054
21 Rooms
Sgl from 141 DM Dbl to 310 DM
Open: All year
Credit Cards: AX, DC, MC
Elegant castle hotel
Ruhr valley
Located 70 km NE of Cologne

An old commercial hotel near the railway station does not seem a likely candidate for inclusion in a book of country inns, but the interior of the hotel is so charming and the nearby old town so picturesque that I could not exclude it.   Limburg is quite a large town but you will have no difficulty finding the Hotel Zimmermann as it is signposted from the time you leave the autobahn.   The hotel is decorated in the prim and proper style of an English Victorian house: dark wood bow-back chairs with deep cushions and velour coverings, prim striped wallpaper and ornate lamps.   Downstairs is a parlor and a dining room, and upstairs are nicely decorated bedrooms, each with its own sitting area.   Triple glazing on the windows eliminates all noise, ensuring a quiet night's sleep.   Mrs Zimmermann cooks dinner only during the week, so on the occasion of my weekend visit, she directed me to the Golden Lion, an atmospheric old German restaurant in the old town where half-timbered houses line narrow cobblestoned pedestrian streets leading to the River Lahn and to one of Germany's most unusual cathedrals.   Seven stories high and ornately painted in coral and white, the cathedral is a splendid example of 13th-century architecture.

HOTEL ZIMMERMANN
Owner: Family Zimmermann
6250 Limburg, Germany
Tel: (06431) 4611 telex: 484782
25 Rooms
Sgl from 86 DM Dbl to 213 DM
Open: All year
Credit Cards: AX, DC, VS
U.S. Rep: Romantik Hotels
Rep. tel: 800-826-0015
Medieval old town
Located 74 km N of Frankfurt

The tiny village of Marienthal is little more than the Haus Elmer, an antique shop and a craft shop clustered around what was once a thriving Augustinian monastery. The hotel is a clever blend of an old and new building. Bedrooms in the old house are smaller and exude country charm; those in the new section are larger and decorated with new country-style furniture. The prettiest bedroom is number two, its beautiful old four-poster bed making it a favorite with honeymooners. There are several dining rooms. One is on the upper story of the new wing and has delightful views of the surrounding countryside through its large picture windows, another is paneled and cozy. The surrounding sky-wide landscapes are perfect for cycling: cyclists pedal easily along, enjoying the country sounds and smells that are lost to speeding motorists. The hotel has plenty of bicycles for you to use during your stay. If you prefer to venture farther afield, the hotel offers a four-night cycling holiday in conjunction with two other hotels in the area. The package includes bicycles, maps, accommodations and the transportation of your luggage from hotel to hotel.

ROMANTIK HOTEL HAUS ELMER
Owner: Karl-Heinz Elmer
4236 Hamminkeln 3
im Ortsteil Marienthal, Germany
Tel: (02856) 2041
28 Rooms
Sgl from 95 DM Dbl to 180 DM
Open: All year
Credit Cards: All major
U.S. Rep: Romantik Hotels
Rep. tel: 800-826-0015
Bicycle tours available
Located 100 km N of Cologne

The Gasthof Zum Baren is a wonderfully atmospheric and friendly old inn located in historic Meersburg, arguably the most picturesque town on Lake Constance. In the Gilowsky family for five generations, the Zum Baren is now smoothly run by young Michael Gilowsky and his attractive wife. Upstairs, a treasure chest of unique bedrooms awaits. Our room had a beautifully carved wooden ceiling, country pine furniture, dainty print wallpaper and lace curtains. Some rooms have old painted furniture and all have antique touches and pretty wallpapers. It is important to note that the Zum Baren is a "gasthof" not a hotel: thus bedrooms are not equipped with telephones or televisions, although all have private bath or shower. Downstairs, the two cozy dining rooms are decorated with pewter plates and typical blue stoneware filling shelves above carved wooden furniture and comfy window benches with pretty print cushions and pillows. A wood parquet floor, low, beamed ceiling and white tile stove add to the pervading feeling of "gemutlichkeit". Both dining rooms contain only large tables for six to eight persons. This is purposely done to encourage guests to share a table, perhaps some wine, and certainly some good conversation. A very warm and charming inn, the Gasthof Zum Baren holds a special place in our hearts.

GASTHOF ZUM BAREN
Owner: Family Gilowsky
Marktplatz 11
7758 Meersburg, Germany
Tel: (07532) 6044
16 Rooms
Sgl from 50 DM Dbl to 100 DM
Closed: November 15 to March 15
Credit Cards: None
Picturesque old town
Located 170 km SE of Stuttgart

On the left bend of the Main river, Miltenberg is a charming mix of cobblestoned streets and sloping slate and tile roofs. It is a quick and rewarding hike up from the market place to the castle ruins for a splendid view overlooking this picturesque village. On Haupstrasse, a street reserved for pedestrians, you will enjoy a number of quaint shops and discover a dear little inn. With its timbered facade and charming decor, the Hotel Zum Riesen has served as a welcome travelers' retreat for close to 400 years, but it has only been the last 15 years that it has profited immensely from the efforts and care of Cilly and Werner Jost. Preserving the weathered beams of the ceilings and walls, the Josts have added plumbing and heating throughout. In each of the 14 rooms the beds are decked with plump down comforters. The decor is further enhanced by some handsome antiques and Oriental rugs cover the hardwood floors. Breakfast is served on the third floor. Easter morning we were greeted with a stunning breakfast setting: tables were laid with fresh linens, candles and flowers, and thoughtfully wrapped Easter gifts were set out for all. Fresh jams, rolls, meats, cheese, juice and an egg were served and Frau Jost was there to welcome and seat her guests - with a warm smile.

HOTEL ZUM RIESEN
Owners: Cilly & Werner Jost
Hauptstrasse 97
8760 Miltenberg, Germany
Tel: (09371) 2582
14 Rooms
Sgl from 71 DM Dbl to 174 DM
Open: Easter to mid November
Credit Cards: DC
Located 160 km SE of Frankfurt

Almost touching the Belgian border, the little town of Monschau hides in a deep ravine. Hugging the banks of the tumbling River Rur, the town is a jumble of tiny picture-perfect houses. Located on the marketplace, the small Muhlen Berg Hotel Weinstube is just as toy-like as the surrounding houses. Downstairs is the wine bar where the owner Herbert Lehnen is the friendly waiter, barman and hotel receptionist. His wife remains behind the scenes producing simple yet well-cooked German food. A steep, narrow staircase winds upstairs to the bedrooms. The higher you climb, the narrower and creakier the stairs. One tiny, less desirable room faces the back of the house. The others face the market place with two on each floor, their low ceilings held up by rough hewn beams. Pretty sprigged papers give a country feel though the furnishings are simple. An added bonus is a gleaming pine whirlpool and solarium tucked into the back of the house on the second floor. A delightful museum to visit while in the town is the Rotes Haus, whose interior remains just the way it was when it was the home of a prosperous 18th-century wool merchant.

MUHLEN BERG HOTEL WEINSTUBE
Owner: Herbert Lehnen
Markt 6
5108 Monschau, Germany
Tel: (02472) 2737 telex: 8329423
7 Rooms
Sgl from 50 DM Dbl to 99 DM
Open: All year
Credit Cards: All major
Exceptionally beautiful town
Whirlpool, solarium
Near the Belgian border
Located 170 km SW of Cologne

The Hotel Blauer Bock dates from 1297 when the original structure was built as a Benedictine chapel. It has been a gasthof since the early 1800s, and today offers up-to-date accommodation and the refreshing Seasons restaurant. The 75 guest rooms vary in furnishings and bath facilities, and about half have recently been refurbished in a very comfortable and tasteful style. Soft colors, paintings, and reproduction antique furniture are combined to create a refined atmosphere. Unrefurbished rooms are likely to be brightly modern and not as comfortable, but the price will be a bargain. The Seasons restaurant welcomes guests through an archway festooned with garlands of dried flowers. The smaller dining room is for lighter meals, a light and airy room with white tile floors, wrought iron chairs, and marble-topped tables. A salad bar with a cornucopia of appetizing selections as well as imaginative sandwiches are offered here. The adjacent room is very attractively decorated with wood paneling, moss green upholstery, fresh flowers and ficus trees. It is a vegetarian's paradise whose menu offers healthy ingredients in a wide variety of unusual, nutritious dishes. A happy discovery, the Hotel Blauer Bock offers a fresh, country hotel atmosphere in the bustling city of Munich.

HOTEL BLAUER BOCK
Owner: Frau Ruhland
Sebastiansplatz 9
8000 Munich, Germany
Tel: (089) 2608043
75 Rooms
Sgl from 53 DM Dbl to 130 DM
Open: All year
Credit Cards: None
Restaurant, parking garage
Located on the Sebastiansplatz, near the old section of Munich

It is rare to experience in a city hotel such gracious, professional, personalized service as you receive at the Preysing Hotel. With 76 rooms, I don't know whether to compare it to Munich's large, elegant establishments or to her small traditional hotels, but either way it achieves the best of both. The bedrooms are furnished with extremely comfortable beds, down comforters covered in pressed white linen, a desk and a few prints. The lighting is excellent and each room has a mini bar and an electrically operated shade that can descend over the window to shut out street noise and light. The bathrooms are thoughtfully equipped with large bath towels, shampoo, toothbrush, toothpaste, hair dryer and sewing kit. Strawberries and a welcome note were placed in my room on the afternoon I arrived and then a different fruit was provided with each additional day. Beds are turned down each night and a sweet is left on the pillow. At the Preysing the service is personalized and attentive, from the chambermaid to the night clerk. The hotel has an excellent restaurant that is open for dinner. A lavish breakfast is served in the downstairs restaurant or on a trolley decked with linen and fresh flowers in the privacy of your room.

PREYSING HOTEL
Owner: Hans Wurbser
Preysingstrasse 1
8000 Munich, Germany
Tel: (089) 481011 telex: 529044
76 Rooms
Sgl from 140 DM Dbl to 255 DM
Open: All year
Located in the nearby suburb of Haidhausen

Old carved wooden angels welcome guests into the lobby of the charming and elegant Hotel Prinz Regent in Munich. This hotel has been open only four years, and, although newly built, it is filled with antique beams, furnishings, and artifacts. Great care has been taken to preserve and exhibit fine Bavarian craftsmanship, and consequently guests are surrounded by artful woodcarvings, wrought iron work, and coffered ceilings. The rustically cozy breakfast room is entirely paneled in warm pine, with an impressive copper topped buffet area where a generous breakfast buffet is served. On summer mornings, the French doors to the garden are opened and guests may enjoy a leisurely outdoor breakfast. There are 67 guest bedrooms, all impeccably furnished in muted colors, with matching curtains, upholstery and bedspreads. All have phone, color television, minibar, and white marble baths with shower and w.c. Most of the rooms are only adequate in size, although some larger king-bedded suites with small sitting areas are also available. The young, energetic and professional staff speak excellent English and are happy to help guests in any way. The Hotel Prinz Regent is an elegant and traditional Bavarian country inn, a real refuge in the bustling city of Munich.

HOTEL PRINZ REGENT
Owner: Biermann Hotels
Manager: Rolf Uhlmann
Ismaninger Strasse 42-44
8000 Munich, Germany
Tel: (089) 416050 telex: 524203
67 Rooms
Sgl from 185 DM Dbl to 260 DM
Closed: December 23 to January 5
Credit Cards: All major
Garden, sauna, parking garage
Located across the Isar River from the old center of Munich

Frau Furholzner solicitously takes guests under her wing at the Pension Schubert, and she spoils them with generous breakfasts and comfortable, spotless rooms. Located on a quiet side street, the atmosphere at the Pension Schubert is not at all hotel-like. There is no lobby or public area to speak of, but if you are looking for homey comfort and a place to rest your head at night, this is a reasonably priced alternative. The pension is found on the second floor of a former villa, thus the rooms are all high-ceilinged and vary in size. Furnishings are a mixture of antiques and contemporary pieces, complemented by pretty drapes and Oriental rugs. Only three of the six rooms have private bath. The foyer displays many family knickknacks and mementos and creates a cheerful, informal atmosphere. The tiny breakfast room has lace covered tables and antique furnishings and is an agreeable place to meet other guests and plan sightseeing excursions for the day. For joggers and travelers who enjoy walking in Europe's city parks, the Theresienweise park is easily found just a block to the west. The Pension Schubert is a good choice for travelers who prefer to spend their time and money outside of their hotel, appreciate a home-like ambiance, and do not require all the services offered in a hotel. However, Frau Furholzner seems to be constantly booked, so early reservations are advised.

PENSION SCHUBERT
Owner: Frau Furholzner
1 Schubertstrasse
8000 Munich, Germany
Tel: (089) 535087
6 Rooms
Sgl from 42 DM Dbl to 78 DM
Open: All year
Credit Cards: None
Located about five blocks S of the main train station

A somewhat sterile city facade hides this traditional and cozy hotel. With the river just to its left and the Marienplatz a few blocks to its rear, the Splendid is an ideally located treasure. The entrance and downstairs salon are inviting, giving only a glimpse of the mood of furnishings to be found in the individualized bedrooms. Oriental carpets enhance hardwood floors, lovely antiques grace the walls and clusters of tables and chairs upholstered in tones of pink make the salon an inviting place to rest after the inevitable city wandering. An outside terrace is a treat on warm days and an ideal spot for tea or an afternoon refreshment. The Splendid does not have a restaurant though a buffet breakfast is offered. This is a small hotel with only 41 bedrooms, but each a jewel with beautifully painted armoirs, traditional to the region of Bavaria, lovely wooden beds, and sitting areas. Everything is spotless, and bathrooms have modern facilities. This hotel is an extremely convenient and comfortable place to reside in Munich and very pleasing to the eye as well. Traditional decor permeates every room - a surprise and unexpected discovery in a large city. A delight.

SPLENDID HOTEL
Maximilianstrasse 54
8000 Munich, Germany
Tel: (089) 296606 telex: 522427
41 Rooms
Sgl from 102 DM Dbl to 302 DM
Open: All year
Credit Cards: AX
Lovely inner courtyard
Located near city center

The Hof Zur Linde is as lovely inside and out as the brochure depicts. It is a complex of old farm buildings connected by courtyards and surrounded by grassy lawns and woodlands leading down to a river.   At dinnertime you can choose from a selection of dining rooms.   These are all actually adjacent, but each has been done in a totally different style so that you move from a light pine-paneled room with gay red gingham curtains where you dine in cozy booths to one with stucco walls and beams, a huge walk-in fireplace, flagstone floors and hams hung from the ceiling.   The main dining room is more formal with its tapestry-covered chairs and starched white linens.   The menu is extensive, the food delicious, and the service friendly and efficient.   Bedrooms are upstairs in the main building or in a lovely old farmhouse just a few steps away.   You may find yourself sleeping in a bed that was made for British royalty or in a rustic pine bed beneath a curtained canopy. Summer mornings find Mr Lofken, the hotel owner, busy selecting bicycles, adjusting saddles, checking tires, and providing maps for guests setting off to explore the area.

ROMANTIK HOTEL HOF ZUR LINDE
Owner: Otta Lofken
Am Handorfer Werseufer 1
4400 Munster, Germany
Tel: (0251) 325002 telex: 891500
30 Rooms
Sgl 98 DM Dbl to 180 DM
Closed: for Christmas
U.S. Rep: Romantik Hotels
Rep. tel: 800-826-0015
Bicycle tours available
Located 164 km NE of Cologne

Just 20 years old, the Alpenhof Murnau is able to provide its guests with luxuriously modern accommodations in a chalet-style building set on the hills near the town of Murnau, a convenient distance to either Oberammergau or the resort town of Garmisch-Partenkirchen. This is a pleasing hotel in the comfortable style and standard of the Relais et Chateaux chain. The hotel has 48 rooms that are all spacious and enjoy patios that overlook either the lake and gardens or onto the hillsides. The furnishings are modern but tasteful (the green doors of each room were my only question as to selection of decor). The Alpenhof Murnau has two principal restaurants, the Reiterzimmer and the Zirbelstube, both overlooking the pool and lake. The Bockbeutelstube is a basement wine room and the Holzkiste is an intimate room to linger over an aperitif. The reception area is tiled and beautifully appointed with beamed ceilings and tapestry covered chairs.

ALPENHOF MURNAU
Owner: Hellmut Hofmann
Ramsachstrasse 8
Am Staffelsee
8110 Murnau, Germany
Tel: (08841) 1045
48 Rooms
Sgl from 135 DM Dbl to 300 DM
Open: All year
U.S. Rep: David Mitchell
Rep. tel: 800-372-1323
Swimming pool
Located 70 km SE of Munich

A hallway full of family antiques leads to a reception desk brightened by a bouquet of fresh flowers at the charming Gasthof Zur Rose in Oberammergau. The gasthof is well located on a quiet street one block from the central square. The friendly and gracious Frau Stuckl welcomes guests to her establishment where she encourages visitors to get to know one another. All her family members are experts on local sights and history, and in fact her talented son is currently the director of the famous Passion Play which takes place every 10 years in Oberammergau. Frau Stuckl's artistic touches are found throughout the Zur Rose, from colorful dried flower arrangements and strategically placed paintings, to pleasing combinations of fabrics. Formerly a farmer's stable, the gasthof is almost 200 years old, and has been in Frau Stuckl's family for 37 years. The two dining rooms are bright and airy, filled with pretty fabrics, rustic furniture, and green plants. The kitchen is much appreciated by guests as it offers Bavarian specialties as well as dishes more familiar to travelers. The 29 bedrooms are simple and pretty, and 10 have private bath. A visit to this antique-filled inn is a delight, enhanced by Frau Stuckl's helpful hospitality.

GASTHOF ZUR ROSE
Owner: Family Stuckl
Dedlerstrasse 9
8103 Oberammergau, Germany
Tel: (08822) 4706 or 4772
29 Rooms
Sgl from 27 DM Dbl to 58 DM
Closed: November
Credit Cards: All major
Beautiful Bavarian village
Located approximately 80 km SW of Munich

"Every room and niche reveals sweet sentiment, fond memories, a blending of both noble craft and art.   Beauty which might adorn a cold museum has found a living home, shared with each guest", a sentiment written in the Haus Wiese guest book. After reading the above, you might be disappointed to find a modern facade.   But do not be misled.   The interior of the Haus Wiese is cozy, filled with art treasures and highlighting the Wieses' own cherished remembrances and furnishings. Before coming to what they consider the most beautiful region in Germany, the Wieses' home was Hamburg.   But the Hotel Wiese is like a small Hamburg in Oberstdorf: the handcrafted and tiled wall scene by the indoor pool, the prints and the etching in the front entry - all depict Hamburg.   Oberstdorf itself is a dear village tucked in the mountains on the Austrian border and the Haus Wiese is a superior little inn.   We went to sleep in a room that overlooked a field of rich green and woke to view an expanse of white snow.   We felt fortunate to experience the village of Oberstdorf in both winter and spring dress.

HAUS WIESE
Owner: Otto & Christa Wiese
Stillachstrasse 4a
8980 Oberstdorf, Germany
Tel: (08322) 3030
13 Rooms
Sgl from 70 DM Dbl to 150 DM
Closed: mid April to mid May
           and November to mid December
Indoor pool
Located 165 km SW of Munich

The Auf Schonburg is the perfect castle hotel.   High atop a rocky bluff, the facade is a fairytale picture of towers and battlements reached by crossing a narrow wooden bridge.   Cobbles worn smooth by feet through the ages wind through the castle to the hotel at the summit.   The terrace view is superb, dropping steeply to the Rhine below.   The bedrooms are shaped by the unusual castle buildings - tower rooms sit atop steep winding staircases while other rooms are tucked neatly into a darling little black and white cottage leaning against the castle wall.   Each bedroom is delightful in its own way: four have romantic four-poster beds, all are furnished with antiques.   Through the tiny lead-paned windows you may be able to catch a glimpse of the River Rhine far below.   However, some of the castle's most beautiful accommodations do not have river views.   The romance extends to the intimate dining rooms where you dine by candlelight.   The terrace restaurant has lovely views to the vineyards while the tower dining room with its displays of pewter and weapons has medieval charm.   Come spin yourself a dream or two in this fairytale castle above the Rhine.

AUF SCHONBURG
Owner: Family Huttl
6532 Oberwesel, Germany
Tel: (06744) 8198
20 Rooms
Sgl from 90 DM Dbl to 220 DM
Open: March to November
Credit Cards: AX, VS
Beautiful castle overlooking Rhine River
Located 95 km W of Frankfurt

The Romantik Hotel Schwan, with its grey tile roof and timbered facade, has been around since 1628 when it was a travelers' inn along the River Rhine. Today both the road and the river in front of the hotel are a lot busier than in the days of carriages and river barges. Fortunately the hotel is saved from being overwhelmed by the busy Rhineside road by a broad band of garden that separates it from the highway. The Wenckstern family has owned and managed the inn for many generations. They produce their own wine which you can sample with dinner in the dignified dining room or sip on the outdoor terrace while watching the river. From a small hostelry, the Schwan has grown to a substantial hotel, and the joy of staying here is that you can obtain a Rhine-facing room. The nicest bedroom is the tower room. Decked out in floral fabric, this circular room commands lovely river views from its seven windows. Incidentally, the Hotel Schwan is only about an hour's drive from the Frankfurt airport, a convenient distance after a tiring transatlantic flight. Its location on the Rheingau Reisling Road makes it especially appealing.

ROMANTIK HOTEL SCHWAN
Owner: Family Wenckstern
Rheinallee 5-7
6227 Oestrich-Winkel, Germany
Tel: (06723) 3001 telex: 42146
66 Rooms
Sgl from 109 DM Dbl to 200 DM
Open: January to November
Credit Cards: All major
U.S. Rep: Romantik Hotels
Rep. tel: 800-826-0015
Located 55 km W of Frankfurt

The town of Passau has a dramatic position at the intersection of three rivers: the Inn, the Ilz and the Danube. The town is built on a rocky peninsula where the swirling waters merge. Small twisting streets weave from the water's edge into a maze of ancient buildings, frequently joined to each other by stone arches. Passau has a strategic position both because of its river traffic and because it is right on the Austrian border. Should you be driving from Austria, or taking the Danube steamer to Vienna, you might be looking for a place to stay. There are no deluxe hotels in Passau, but the Schloss Ort is splendidly located. Although the decor has no olde worlde charm (plastics and modern furniture prevail), the building itself is very old and quite attractive. The Danube, Inn and Ilz rivers all meet and flow below a number of the bedroom windows and the terrace and indoor restaurants enjoy views of passing boat traffic. Tucked on a small side street, amid the stone walls of the original castle, the 35 bedrooms of the Schloss Ort are quiet and comfortable, although, like the public rooms, quite plain in their decor and furnishings. The management and service are efficient if not overly personal.

SCHLOSS ORT
Owner: Heinrich Detzer
Im Ort 11, am Dreiflusseck
8390 Passau, Germany
Tel: (0851) 34072
35 Rooms
Sgl from 40 DM Dbl to 100 DM
Closed: January and February
Near dock for Danube excursions
Located on the Austrian border

Originally a postal station, this inn has always been under the management of the Pflaum family. Two brothers, Andreas and Hermann Pflaum, continue the family tradition. The oldest room to serve travelers food still exists as the beer tavern: adjoining is a more formal restaurant. A lovely bar whose few tables are set and warmed before an open fire also offers piano music on Friday and Saturday evenings. The bedrooms are an interesting melange of modern to cozy antique. Down a very narrow, timbered corridor in the original building are sixteen rooms, decorated in delightful country prints and beautiful antiques. A newer wing provides guests a choice of accommodations in a modern as well as traditional decor. The newer wing also affords a few discreetly placed conference rooms, a kegelgahnen (similar to a bowling alley), a lovely large swimming pool, sauna, solarium and massage facilities.

PFLAUM'S POSTHOTEL
Owner: Andreas & Hermann Pflaum
Nurnberger Strasse 14
8570 Pegnitz, Germany
Tel: (09241) 7250 telex: 642433
50 Rooms
Sgl from 126 DM Dbl to 305 DM
Open: All year
Credit Cards: All major
U.S. Rep: David Mitchell
Rep. tel: 800-372-1323
Swimming pool, sauna, bowling
Located 206 km N of Munich

A local woman directed me to the Bavaria Hotel by pointing across to a dominating mountain and stating that at its base I would find the Bavaria. She spoke with a heavy German accent and referred to the hotel as if it were a local tradition. I was therefore surprised to find a very modern facade and then glad to discover a traditional and warm interior. If you are lucky, Herr Hoff might even be at the front desk, dressed in lederhosen, to greet you personally. The lobby is lovely with plants, beams and a big open fireplace. There is a small attractive restaurant for a la carte dining and a bar off the main lobby. An exceptionally lovely room, paneled in light wood, furnished with heart-carved wooden chairs and country prints, is reserved for pension guests. Located in a sport and health region, the hotel has both an outdoor and indoor pool, sauna, and a lounge area shaded by white umbrellas and greenery. The bedrooms are very handsome in furnishings and very modern in comfort. You have the choice of a bedroom with loft, a "galeria studio" - a room with sitting area, an apartment that has a separate living room and studio, or a basic double bedded room. Many of the rooms have cozy fireplaces, all have private bathrooms and most have their own balcony or terrace.

BAVARIA HOTEL
Owner: Georg Hoff
Kienbergstrasse 62
8962 Pfronten-Dorf, Germany
Tel: (08363) 5004
50 Rooms
Sgl from 85 DM Dbl to 260 DM
Closed: November to mid December
Swimming pool, sauna
Located 131 km SW of Munich

If you are arriving at or departing from Hamburg airport and have a car, the Jagdhaus Waldfrieden makes a splendid overnight for your first or last night in Germany. Isolated by its parklike setting and the surrounding woodlands, the hotel has that special quiet atmosphere found only in country house hotels. During the course of his career as the manager of large hotels, Siegmund Baierle formulated his plans for a small hotel with a first-rate restaurant - the result is the delightful Jagdhaus Waldfrieden. You step from the tiny reception and bar area to the dining room whose ceiling soars to the eaves of the house. Gleaming polished wood, Oriental carpets and groupings of tables laid with crisp white linen before a roaring log fire create a stylish atmosphere while guests enjoy splendid dinners. These evening-long affairs find the guests lingering at their tables before retiring for a contented night's sleep. A few bedrooms are found in the main building and the remainder are across the courtyard in what was once the stables Their decor is almost identical, smart and tailored on a classic theme.

JAGDHAUS WALDFRIEDEN
Owner: Siegmund Baierle
2085 Quickborn, Germany
Tel: (04106) 3771
17 Rooms
Sgl from 85 DM Dbl to 175 DM
Open: All year
Credit Cards: All major
U.S. Rep: Romantik Hotels
Rep. tel: 800-826-0015
Hunting lodge
Located 23 km N of Hamburg

"Gast im Schloss" (guest in a castle) is a term that almost always guarantees an adventure, but not always a comfortable night's accommodation.   All too often the knights in armor are ever present, but not the firm mattress and the welcome hot and cold running water.   On the River Neckar there are a number of castle hotels which are fun to visit, but the one that I prefer because of the accommodations and cuisine is the Schloss Heinsheim.   Set in parklike grounds, the hotel is surrounded by a forest and has all the ambiance of a large country estate.   Horses frequently frolic in the fields visible from your bedroom window, enhancing the "country mood".   There is a small circular pool that is favored by children and a lovely terraced area set with tables for enjoying meals outside in warm weather.   Inside are two attractive restaurants: one is in a rustic decor and one is a bit more modern. The rooms above the restaurants are furnished quite simply, but those in the building that fronts the circular drive are more spacious and traditional in decor. This romantic hotel is frequently the site of wedding parties, so, with a little luck, you might see a beautiful young bride and her handsome husband.

SCHLOSS HEINSHEIM
Owner: Family Racknitz
6927 Bad-Rappenau, Germany
Tel: (07264) 1045 telex: 782376
40 Rooms
Sgl from 84 DM Dbl to 170 DM
Closed: last 3 weeks of January
Small swimming pool
Located 74 km N of Stuttgart

The Adam Hotel's character and charm are representative of its owner, Herr Adam. He advertises the hotel as "fur Menschen mit Herz", "for people with heart". This little inn is located at the far end of town on a quaint side street just before the Burg Gasse, an easy walk from the center of the village. The Adam Das Kleine Hotel is favored by many who have come to know, understand and love the temperament of its owner. Herr Adam, your host and also your chef, will prepare his version of a gastronomic meal and then offer you the secret of his recipes in the form of cookbooks (for sale, of course). The restaurant is only for hotel guests and the evening meal is at the selection of Herr Adam. The bedrooms, a mix of cherished tidbits and lovely furnishings, are found up a steep, narrow, winding stairway. We were pampered with the large "honeymoon" suite, an especially appealing room with a wall of lead-paned windows looking out onto the castle gardens - a romantic view in one of the most romantic towns in Germany. Herr Adam is a personable man, particularly if you praise his cuisine. For breakfast you can order anything you want as long as you are willing to pay for the extras a la carte.

ADAM DAS KLEINE HOTEL
Owner: H.V. Adam
Burggasse 29
8803 Rothenburg, Germany
Tel: (09861) 2364
20 Rooms
Sgl from 80 DM Dbl to 130 DM
Open: Easter to October
Delightful town on the Romantic Road
Located 140 km SE of Frankfurt

The Gasthof Hotel Kloster-Stuble is a perfect little inn, combining reasonable prices with history, charm, and a good location. Just two blocks from the central market square of Rothenburg ob der Tauber, the Kloster-Stuble is tucked away on a side street behind an old church. This tranquil location affords a restful night's sleep and pretty views of the surrounding countryside from most bedroom windows. Twelve comfortable bedrooms are offered here, all with private shower and w.c. and furnished in beautiful country pine reproductions. Downstairs, the dining room and "stube" are cozily rustic. Murals depicting life in days gone by decorate the stube walls, while in the adjoining dining room pretty rose colored walls and tablecloths set a romantic tone. Tables are dressed with gleaming silver, china and glassware, topped off with pink candles and fresh flowers. French doors lead out onto two lovely terraces which enjoy a scenic view of church spires and distant hills. A sense of history prevails in this inn dating from 1300. Old duck decoys are displayed in a pretty pine hutch in the entryway, and country antique touches add atmosphere throughout. Rudolf Hammel is the young, energetic host at the Kloster-Stuble who does an admirable job attending to guests' needs as well as chef's duties.

GASTHOF HOTEL KLOSTER-STUBLE
Owner: Rudolf Hammel
Heringsbronnengassechen 5
8803 Rothenburg, Germany
Tel: (09861) 6774
12 Rooms
Sgl from 45 DM Dbl to 90 DM
Closed: January and February
Credit Cards: All major
Delightful town on the Romantic Road
Located 140 km SE of Frankfurt

Rothenburg is a fairytale town whose atmosphere is that of the Middle Ages. Completely enclosed by ramparts, walls and turrets, it is a popular destination of many and therefore, regardless of the season, it is often difficult to secure reservations.   To overnight in the city, however, is to experience the best of its charm, as the early morning and evening light and quiet are gentle on the town's cobblestoned streets and timbered facades.   The Markusturm reserves one of the town's best locations, on a main street, just a block or two from the main square and famous clock.   Managed by the Berger family, the hotel was built in 1264 as a tollhouse, converted in 1488 to a brewery, and has been a hotel since 1902.   The entry and restaurant are charmingly decorated with antiques.   The decor in the hallways and public rooms is traditional but the rooms range from very modern to the favorite four-poster room.   I was able to see only a few of the bedrooms as the hotel was fully occupied, but I will rely on the recommendation of many and include this hotel, having acquainted myself with the Berger hospitality and the olde worlde ambiance of the public rooms.

ROMANTIK HOTEL MARKUSTURM
Owner: Marianne Berger
Rodergasse 1
8803 Rothenburg, Germany
Tel: (09861) 2370
26 Rooms
Sgl from 130 DM Dbl to 250 DM
Closed: mid January to mid March
Credit Cards: AX, DC, MC
U.S. Rep: Romantik Hotels
Rep. tel: 800-826-0015
Delightful town on the Romantic Road
Located 140 km SE of Frankfurt

This is it - Sleeping Beauty's Castle.   Here, deep within the "enchanted" Reinhard forest, Jacob and Wilhelm Grimm set their famous fairytale.   What was once a proud fortress is now largely a romantic ruin - a shell of towers and walls. Fortunately one wing has been restored as a hotel.   The romance of staying in Sleeping Beauty's Castle cannot be denied, but be aware that the isolated location does not invite a long stay.   There is no lounge or bar to gather in before or after dinner, so splurge and request a larger room.   Tables in the dining room are assigned by management: the only way to ensure a lovely countryside view is to request a window table as you check in.   The house specialty is mouthwatering venison.   If you are familiar with Walt Disney's Sleeping Beauty Castle, be prepared for a disappointment, for this is not it: he chose the ethereal towers and turrets of Neuschwanstein Castle in Bavaria as his model.   In honor of the Brothers Grimm and their world-famous tales, the German Tourist Office has outlined a fairytale route, the "Deutsche Marchen Strasse", signposted by a smiling good fairy and accompanied by a colorful picture map.   The Burghotel Sababurg is included on this routing and as a consequence is a popular tourist attraction.   Plan on arriving quite late in the afternoon after the coachloads of daytime visitors have left.

BURGHOTEL SABABURG
Owner: K. Koseck & S. Horgeismar
3520 Sababurg-Hofgeismar, Germany
Tel: (05678) 1052 1055
19 Rooms
Sgl from 74 DM Dbl to 189 DM
Sleeping Beauty's Castle
Located 300 km S of Hamburg

In the Black Forest on a hillside in the town of Schluchsee is a delightful, modern hotel. Constructed in 1969 with a new wing added in 1984, Heger's Parkhotel Flora is beautiful in its decor and in the views that it affords down to the Schluchsee. Each room has been charmingly furnished and all overlook the lake: views can be enjoyed from either a private balcony or terrace. The hallways are beamed, spacious and airy, with floor to ceiling windows. The public rooms are attractive with colorful prints on the walls, wrought iron fixtures, plants, and pink and green fabrics. Herr Heger, dressed impeccably in chef's attire, is frequently found in the lobby to greet guests, and as eager to make you comfortable as he is to please and tempt your palate. The "St Georgstube" and the cafe-terrace restaurant are delightful. The entry hall with its open fireplace is a cozy place to settle in inclement weather. In warm summer weather the Schluchsee comes alive with the sails of gay colored sailing boats and wind surfers.

HEGER'S PARKHOTEL FLORA
Owner: Herr Heger
Sonnhalde 22
7826 Schluchsee, Germany
Tel: (07656) 452
34 Rooms
Sgl from 82 DM Dbl to 168 DM
Closed: November to Christmas
New hotel with charm
Lovely lake views
Located 172 km S of Stuttgart

The Hotel Goldener Adler is managed by the Rapp family. This very ancient building, in bygone days a postal stop, has a mix of modern and traditionally furnished rooms, some of which also enjoy a bird's eye view of the square. (Note that this can be a disadvantage on a noisy weekend night.) You can order light meals on the terrace of the outdoor cafe or enjoy a more formal presentation of lunch or dinner in the hotel's fine restaurant. The entrance to the hotel is through gigantic doors, reminders of the era when horse-drawn coaches would come clomping through the portals. Inside, the hotel is quite simple. Most of the bedrooms are very basic but a few are especially large and have some antique furnishings which, although rather fussy, have character. Schwabisch Hall is an outstanding medieval town - comparable in many ways to the much better known walled town of Rothenburg which is on every tourist route. The central plaza is one of the prettiest in Germany and always teeming with activity - a "real town" with women carefully selecting their produce for the evening meal from small stalls in the square and children neatly dressed in uniforms gaily chatting on their way to school. The prime objective in coming to Schwabisch Hall should be to soak in the wonderful ambiance of this lovely old city - and for this, the Hotel Goldener Adler could not be more ideally located.

HOTEL GOLDENER ADLER
Owner: Marion & Peter Rapp
Am Marktplatz 11
7170 Schwabisch Hall, Germany
Tel: (0791) 6168
20 Rooms
Sgl from 65 DM Dbl to 130 DM
Colorful medieval town
Located 68 km NE of Stuttgart

Schwabisch Hall is an atmospheric town not far from the ever-popular Romantische Strasse (Romantic Road), yet profiting from the fact that it is not as heavily visited and is able to retain its atmosphere, character and charm. Set on two sides of the Neckar river, the town boasts picturesque covered bridges, old timbered houses that lean over and threaten to tumble onto narrow passageways, and some lovely cathedrals. It is a fun town to explore and at lunchtime offers a tempting variety of sidewalk cafes for dining or grassy lawns for picnicking. The Ratskeller Hotel, ideally located in the center of town, has a very austere cold stone exterior but utilizes in all its public areas a wealth of antiques and traditional furnishings. The bedrooms vary from functional modern to very country in decor. One should definitely specify a preference for decor when making reservations. The Haupt restaurant is staged to create a medieval mood and the Candlelight Restaurant, as the name implies, is for an intimate evening. The hotel service and staff are very professional and accommodating.

RATSKELLER HOTEL
Owner: Alois Hager
Am Markt 12-13
7170 Schwabisch Hall, Germany
Tel: (0791) 6181 telex: 74893
46 Rooms
Sgl from 74 DM Dbl to 182 DM
Open: All year
Credit Cards: VS, DC, AX
Modern exterior but nice inside
Heart of medieval town
Located 68 km NE of Stuttgart

The friendly Heim family has been welcoming guests into their home since 1959 and Herr Heim still keeps the old guest books filled with entries and artwork by former guests. Believe it or not, some of the original guests still visit the Pension Heim, but now they are accompanied by children and even grandchildren. Herr Heim was originally a cheesemaker by trade, and in fact he is featured in the local cheese museum. However, he had to choose another profession, and so opened this pension which gradually grew year by year due to demand. It is easy to see why guest numbers continued to increase, as the entire family is warm and genuine and the house spotless and homey. Cheerful houseplants brighten all the rooms and hallways and a rustic feeling pervades the dining rooms and "stube". Home-cooked meals are offered if guests so desire, and the ambiance is very convivial, fostering many new friendships. Upstairs, most of the comfortable bedrooms have balconies which overlook spectacularly unspoilt mountain scenery, even offering a glimpse of the famous Zugspitze on a clear day. The rolling hills and pastures of this region make it ideal for relaxed hiking in the summer and cross country skiing in the winter. Pension Heim offers comforts such as private bath or shower in each room, direct dial phones, and even a sauna. Just the right ending to a day of enjoying all the activities that this scenic area has to offer.

PENSION HEIM
Owner: Family Heim
Aufmberg/Ostallgau
8959 Seeg, Germany
Tel: (08364) 258
18 Rooms
Sgl from 45 DM Dbl to 98 DM
Closed: November to December 20
Credit Cards: None
Located 120 km SW of Munich, just N of Fussen

Come dream a romantic dream or two at the lovely Schloss Spangenberg. High atop a hill with the town of Spangenberg spread at its feet far below, this once proud fortress is now a delightful castle hotel. All the romantic castle ingredients are here - a deep grassy moat, a tower keep and thick fortified walls. With seven centuries of embattled history, this fortification was badly damaged by British bombers in the closing days of World War II. Like so many historic buildings, the exterior has been painstakingly reconstructed. With great ingenuity, the once cold interior has been turned into an inviting hotel. A few steps away, where soldiers once guarded the ramparts, gay tables and chairs now provide a perfect place for afternoon coffee and cake. Gleaming polished floors lead you down the long hallways to the bedrooms, which, papered and pretty, offer a warm welcome. The decor is all old-fashioned, but over the years decorators have left their mark - some preferred the French look, others the heavy Victorian. Only the more recent room renovations reflect a romantic German-castle feeling. My favorite room lies outside the castle walls, in a dear little gatekeeper's house. Comprising a doll-sized living room, sleeping loft, tiny bedroom and two bathrooms, it is perfect for families or a group of friends traveling together.

SCHLOSS SPANGENBERG
Owner: Family Wichmann
3509 Spangenberg, Germany
Tel: (05663) 866
26 Rooms
Sgl from 75 DM Dbl to 180 DM
Open: February to December
Credit Cards: All major
Located 210 km S of Hamburg

The Hotel Traube, conveniently located across the expressway from the Stuttgart airport, is a beguiling little inn. Should you be flying into Stuttgart to visit the Mercedes factory and perhaps pick up a car, the Hotel Traube would be an excellent choice for a place to spend the night since the factory is only a short drive from the hotel. The contrast between this small inn and the modern industrial city of Stuttgart, located only about a half hour's drive away, is dramatic. Located on a small cobblestoned square, contained in a cluster of three timbered buildings, the Hotel Traube would stand out as a perfect inn regardless of its location. Michelin has awarded the hotel's kitchen a star, the highest rating to be found in the city, and I would give the decor of the restaurant a rating of multiple stars. Tables laid with soft pink cloths, flowers and candles are tucked under beams into cozy corners paneled in rich wood. If you'd prefer less formal dining, consider the neighboring rotisserie, managed by the gracious son and daughter who maintain the same high standards set by their parents. The rotisserie has a welcoming bar and a lighter fare on the menu, letting you select from different cuts of meat grilled on the open barbecue. The guest rooms, located far enough away from the street to be quiet, are most attractive with traditional decor and comfortable beds topped with fluffy down comforters.

HOTEL TRAUBE
Owner: Family Recknagel
Brabandtgasse 2
7000 Stuttgart-Plieningen, Germany
Tel: (0711) 454833
22 Rooms
Sgl from 73 DM Dbl to 210 DM
Closed: Christmas and New Year
Excellent restaurant
Located near Stuttgart airport

Cuckoo clocks and fabulous Black Forest trails are the initial draws to the popular town of Triberg. The Parkhotel Wehrle is the reason for one's return. An ivy-covered yellow stone building, the Wehrle occupies a corner position on the main street of Triberg. For those fortunate enough to have the Wehrle as a base for travels, you will experience the professional care and welcome of Herr and Frau Claus Blum, the warmth of their hotel and the excellence of their restaurant. The hotel, originally named the Golden Ox, was built in 1707, and has been owned and managed by the same family since then. Bedrooms in the main building are spacious and traditional in their furnishings. An annex with attractive modern rooms, built approximately fifteen years ago, houses an unusually attractive indoor swimming pool, sauna and jacuzzi. The Parkhotel Wehrle, in conjunction with neighboring hotels, has a plan whereby you can walk between hotels located 12 to 17 miles apart. You need only carry your picnic lunch because your luggage is transferred to your next destination.

PARKHOTEL WEHRLE
Owner: Family Blum-Wehrle
Gartenstrasse 24
7740 Triberg, Germany
Tel: (07722) 86020 telex: 792609
60 Rooms
Sgl from 80 DM Dbl to 250 DM
Open: All year
Credit Cards: VS, DC,
U.S. Rep: Romantik Hotels
Rep. tel: 800-226-0015
Swimming pool, sauna
Located 139 km SW of Stuttgart

The exterior of the Romantik Hotel Menzhausen is a 16th-century dazzler: its facade half timbered, with painted decorations. Found on the main street of this attractive town, the Hotel Menzhausen has been offering travelers lodging for over 400 years. Like so many tiny town hostelries, the hotel has needed to expand and has done so by adding a modern extension of 20 bedrooms at the rear of the building. Decorated in a modern style, these rooms are rather bland. I was unable to see any of the older rooms as they were all occupied, but Fritz Korber, the owner, assured me that they are decorated in keeping with the historic core of the hotel. Mr Korber's special pride is his wine cellar and he will be happy to show you around. It is great fun to follow him down the low, narrow, dark, brick passage into the cellars lined with neat rows of bottles. The dining room is delightful: roughhewn beams and country charm or polished light pine contrasting with gay red and white checked tablecloths. Uslar features on the "Deutsche Marchen Strasse", or "Fairytale Route", signposted by a smiling fairy inviting you to follow her down the fairytale road.

ROMANTIK HOTEL MENZHAUSEN
Owner: Fritz Korber
Lange Strasse 12
3418 Uslar, Germany
Tel: (05571) 2051
28 Rooms
Sgl from 85 DM Dbl to 138 DM
Open: All year
Credit Cards: All major
U.S. Rep: Romantik Hotels
Rep. tel: 800-826-0015
Located 280 km S of Hamburg

The Hotel Alte Post and Hotel Villa are two hotels in Wangen that benefit from the management and service of Werner and Thomas Veile.   In the heart of the old village, opening onto a cobblestoned square, the Alte Post was built in 1409 as a posting station and is now one of the oldest hotels in Germany.   Horses were stabled below the existing building and exchanged for the next postal journey. Rooms on the first level are devoted to the restaurants of the hotel.   As you climb the stairs to the various bedrooms, the carpets appear a bit worn but everything is spotlessly clean, and polished and scrubbed daily.   Individually decorated by Frau Veile, the style of the rooms varies from comfortable contemporary to richly traditional.   From the third floor guest rooms, tucked under beamed ceilings, you can hear the peal of the nearby church bells.   The Hotel Villa is a large, converted home located on the town's outskirts.   The Villa has three single rooms, four double rooms and a spacious apartment.   A breakfast buffet is the only meal available and is served in a lovely dining room warmed by an open fire in winter and on an outdoor terrace in summer.

ROMANTIK HOTEL ALTE POST & VILLA
Owner: Werner Veile
Postplatz 2
7988 Wangen im Allgau, Germany
Tel: (07522) 4014 telex: 732774
32 Rooms
Sgl from 86 DM Dbl to 170 DM
Open: All year
Credit Cards: All major
U.S. Rep: Romantik Hotels
Rep. tel: 800-826-0015
Located 194 km S of Stuttgart

Use the Hotel Weisserhof as your marker and turn left in the resort village of Bad Wiessee to the small residential district of Sapplfeld and the modern, attractive Landhaus Sapplfeld. Christian Klumpp and his family are your hosts and he as chef will both supervise and perfect the menu. The restaurant is available only to overnight guests, a policy which proves an added incentive for choosing this small hotel. The hotel has seventeen rooms which, although a bit sterile in their light wooden, almost Danish-modern decor, are comfortably furnished, all with either private bath or shower. The doors are decorated with regional handpainted designs and the hallways are attractively hung with tapestries and paintings. In addition to an intimate and cozy restaurant, the Landhaus Sapplfeld also has a cheerful and bright breakfast room and downstairs a beer tavern where one can drink along with the jovial men depicted in a mural on the wall. There is an indoor swimming pool, and from the top of the town's eighteen-hole golf course are some of the region's most spectacular vistas.

LANDHAUS SAPPLFELD
Owner: Christian Klumpp
Im Sapplfeld 8
8182 Bad Wiessee, Germany
Tel: (08022) 82067
17 Rooms
Sgl from 84 DM Dbl to 199 DM
Closed: mid November to mid December
Indoor swimming pool
Located 54 km SE of Munich

Wirsberg is a village just off the autoroute north of Bayreuth. The Romantik Hotel Post, found on the village's main square, was once a posting station. Although part of the hotel appears modern, the reception area and hallway are set under heavy beams and there is a cozy little room tucked back into a corner with leaded glass windows where breakfast is served. For lunch or evening meals the hotel's Patrizier salon is an elegantly set restaurant, while the Jagerstube affords an environment for a more casual rendezvous, beer or supper. For overnight guests, the Herrmann family's wish is to see to all their comforts and create an atmosphere that will tempt them to linger: "Gastlichkeit mit Herz", "hospitality with heart". The bedrooms range in decor from comfortable modern to an attractive traditional, but all are with private bath, superb in facilities and comfort. Also available to hotel guests is the use of a pool styled after a Roman bath, sauna, fitness room, solarium and massage. Werna and Herta Herrmann are the fifth generation of the Herrmann family to offer a warm welcome to guests at the Romantik Hotel Post.

ROMANTIK HOTEL POST
Owner: Werner & Herta Herrmann
Marktplatz 11
8655 Wirsberg, Germany
Tel: (08227) 861 telex: 642906
45 Rooms
Sgl from 68 DM Dbl to 330 DM
Open: All year
Credit Cards: AX, DC,
U.S. Rep: Romantik Hotels
Rep. tel: 800-826-0015
Swimming pool, sauna, solarium
Located 250 km N of Munich

It is difficult to pinpoint the best feature of the Gasthof Hecht because one must choose between its abundant country charm, wonderfully warm and friendly hosts, and extremely reasonable rates. The 300-year-old gasthof is located on the picturesque main street and square of Wolfach where its half-timbered facade overflowing with vari-colored geraniums has long been a welcome sight for travelers. The ground floor contains two atmospheric dining rooms with pewter and pottery collections, beamed ceilings, wood paneled walls and fresh flower bouquets. A friendly neighborhood gathering was in progress when we arrived, adding to the convivial ambiance. Leave your diet at home, as traditional, home-style meals are served here including pork and veal dishes, plenty of vegetables and mouthwatering tortes for dessert. We were ushered to our contemporarily furnished and very clean bedroom by one of the Sattlers' three personable sons. Of the 17 guest bedrooms, all have private bath or shower. The homey upstairs hallways are rich with family antique pieces and Oriental rugs, reflecting the good taste of the Sattler family who also live here. A guest at the Gasthof Hecht truly has the feeling of visiting a private home rather than a hotel.

GASTHOF HECHT
Owner: Klaus Sattler
7620 Wolfach
Schwarzwald, Germany
Tel: (07834) 538
17 Rooms
Sgl from 36 DM Dbl to 74 DM
Closed: January 8 to February 8
Credit Cards: None
Restaurant, television room
Located 40 km NE of Freiburg

Hotel Descriptions 219

A picturesque drive past green meadows and flower bedecked chalets leads to the lovely Gasthof Hirschen in the tiny hamlet of Oberwolfach-Walke. Healthy geraniums adorn the Hirschen's many windowboxes, and a small stream flows by across the street. Full of country charm, the Hirschen dates from 1609 and is one of the oldest inns in the Black Forest. Its picturesque dining room is filled with antique items, fresh flowers and waitresses wearing the traditional dirndl. The menu is enticing, offering a delicious variety of local dishes. Follow the Oriental rug runners up the old staircase to the first floor lobby area which displays an antique clock, sitting area with a huge vase of purple daisies, and a doll cabinet filled with antique dolls. There are 17 guest rooms, all of which have private bath. The rooms are not overly large, but are charmingly furnished and very clean. Apartments are also available in a nearby annex. Sunny days are enjoyed on the flower filled terrace or in the tranquil garden, the only audible sound the birds in surrounding trees. In winter cross country skiing is a popular sport in this region of forests and rolling hills. From its quiet rural location to the warm welcome of the Junghanns family, it is easy to see why the Gasthof Hirschen is a popular country inn for travelers "in the know".

GASTHOF HIRSCHEN
Owner· Family Junghanns
7620 Oberwolfach-Walke, Germany
Tel: (07834) 366
17 Rooms
Sgl from 40 DM Dbl to 88 DM
Closed: three weeks in November
Credit Cards: All major
Sauna, solarium, indoor bowling
Located 5 km N of Wolfach which is 40 km NE of Freiburg

Sehr geehrte Herren,
Dear Sirs,

Wir (Ich) benotigen vom _____ _____ 19__
We (I) wish to reserve as of   *day*   *month*   *year*   *(arrival date)*

bis zum _____ _____ 19__
until   *day*   *month*   *year*   *(departure date)*

_____ Zimmer mit Bad / Dusche
number of rooms with private bath / shower

_____ Zimmer mit Bad / Dusche am Gang,
number of room(s) with bath / shower down the hall,

fur _____ Erwachsene mit _____ Kind(er).
for number of adults with number of children.

Wir mochten:
We would like:

☐ nur Zimmer mit Frustuck
room(s) with breakfast only

☐ mit Halbpension
with breakfast and either lunch or dinner

☐ mit Vollpension
with all meals

Bitte lassen Sie mich wissen, ob Sie etwas zu der gewunschten Zeit frei haben, in welcher Preislage, und ob Anzahlung notwendig ist.

Please let me know if you have a room available, in what price range and if a deposit is required.

Ich danke Ihnen im Voraus.
Thanking you in advance,

Mit freundlichen Grussen,
With friendly greetings,

YOUR NAME AND ADDRESS

Index

Index - Alphabetical Listing by Town

Index - Alphabetical Listing by Town   223

Index - Alphabetical Listing by Town

Index

Index - Alphabetical Listing by Hotel

Hotel	Town	Map	Pages(s)
SCHLOSS HOTEL GRUNWALD	*Grunwald*	*67*	*163*
ROMANTIK HOTEL HAUS ELMER	*Marienthal*	*7*	*184*
HOTEL HAUS LIPMANN	*Beilstein*	*21*	*134*
HAUS LYSKIRCHEN	*Cologne*	*9*	*22 148*
HAUS WIESE	*Oberstdorf*	*60*	*98 196*
GASTHOF HECHT	*Wolfach*	*49*	*219*
HEGER'S PARKHOTEL FLORA	*Schluchsee*	*56*	*208*
PENSION HEIM	*Seeg*	*62*	*211*
SCHLOSS HEINSHEIM	*Bad Rappenau*	*44*	*203*
HINCHLEY WOOD	*Kampen-Sylt*	*2*	*180*
HOTEL ZUM HIRSCH	*Baden Baden*	*47*	*130*
GASTHOF HIRSCHEN	*Wolfach*	*49*	*220*
HOTEL HISTORISCHE BERGMUHLE	*Horbruch*	*23*	*62 176*
ROMANTIK HOTEL HOF ZUR LINDE	*Munster-Handorf*	*6*	*193*
SCHLOSS HUGENPOET	*Kettwig*	*8*	*182*
JAGDHAUS WALDFRIEDEN	*Quickborn*	*4*	*202*
HOTEL KAISERWORTH	*Goslar*	*14*	*121 162*
GASTHOF HOTEL KLOSTER-STUBLE	*Rothenburg*	*41*	*205*
SCHLOSS HOTEL KRONBERG	*Frankfurt*	*27*	*155*
HOTEL KRONE	*Assmannshausen*	*25*	*24 127*
LANDHAUS SAPPLFELD	*Bad Wiessee*	*69*	*217*
ROMANTIK HOTEL MARKUSTURM	*Rothenburg*	*41*	*34 206*
ROMANTIK HOTEL MENZHAUZEN	*Uslar*	*13*	*215*
MONCH'S POSTHOTEL	*Bad Herrenalb*	*46*	*50 171*
MUHLEN BERG HOTEL WEINSTUBE	*Monschau*	*10*	*187*
OBERKIRCH'S WEINSTUBEN	*Freiburg*	*52*	*43 156*
SCHLOSS ORT	*Passau*	*73*	*199*
PARK HOTEL ADLER	*Hinterzarten*	*55*	*173*
POSTHOTEL PARTENKIRCHEN	*Garmisch Partenkirchen*	*64*	*93 161*
PFLAUM'S POSTHOTEL	*Pegnitz*	*36*	*200*
HOTEL ZUR POST	*Bernkastel*	*22*	*140*
ROMANTIK HOTEL POST	*Wirsberg*	*34*	*218*
HOTEL PREM	*Hamburg*	*5*	*102 165*

Index - Alphabetical Listing by Hotel

Hotel	Town	Map	Pages(s)	
PREYSING HOTEL	*Munich*	*66*	*85*	*189*
HOTEL PRINZ REGENT	*Munich*	*66*		*190*
HOTEL GASTHOF ZUM RABEN	*Haslach*	*48*		*166*
RATSKELLER HOTEL	*Schwabisch Hall*	*40*	*75*	*210*
HOTEL REICHSPOST	*Heidelberg*	*29*		*169*
HOTEL ZUM RIESEN	*Miltenberg*	*31*		*186*
HOTEL ZUM RITTER	*Heidelberg*	*29*	*25 78*	*170*
GASTHOF ZUR ROSE	*Oberammergau*	*63*		*195*
BURGHOTEL SABABURG	*Sababurg*	*12*	*117*	*207*
SASSENHOF	*Hinterzarten*	*55*		*174*
DER SCHAFHOF	*Amorbach*	*30*	*69*	*125*
LANDHOTEL SCHINDLERHOF	*Boxdorf*	*37*		*142*
BURGHOTEL SCHNELLENBERG	*Attendorn*	*11*		*128*
AUF SCHONBURG	*Oberwesel*	*24*		*197*
PENSION SCHUBERT	*Munich*	*66*		*191*
ROMANTIK HOTEL SCHWAN	*Oestrich-Winkel*	*26*	*58*	*198*
ROMANTIK HOTEL SONNE	*Badenweiler*	*54*		*131*
SCHLOSS SPANGENBERG	*Spangenberg*	*16*		*212*
SPLENDID HOTEL	*Munich*	*66*	*27*	*192*
HOTEL ZUM STERN	*Bad Hersfeld*	*17*	*114*	*172*
ROMANTIK HOTEL ZUR TANNE	*Braunlage*	*15*	*119*	*144*
SCHLOSS HOTEL THIERGARTEN	*Bayreuth*	*35*		*133*
HOTEL TOPFERHAUS	*Alt Duvenstedt*	*3*	*105*	*124*
HOTEL TRAUBE	*Stuttgart*	*45*		*213*
HOTEL WATZMANN	*Berchtesgaden*	*71*		*136*
PARKHOTEL WEHRLE	*Triberg*	*50*	*47*	*214*
ROMANTIK WEINHAUS MESSERSCHMITT	*Bamberg*	*33*		*132*
HOTEL ZUM WEISSEN SCHWANEN	*Braubach*	*19*		*143*
ROMANTIK HOTEL ZEHNTKELLER	*Iphofen*	*32*		*177*
HOTEL ZIMMERMANN	*Limberg*	*18*		*183*
HOTEL AM ZOO	*Berlin*	*1*		*138*

INN DISCOVERIES FROM OUR READERS

Future editions of *KAREN BROWN'S COUNTRY INN GUIDES* are going to include a new feature - a list of hotels recommended by our readers. We have received many letters describing wonderful inns you have discovered; however, we have never included them until we had the opportunity to make a personal inspection. This seemed a waste of some marvelous "tips". Therefore, in order to feature them we have decided to add a new section called "Inn Discoveries from Our Readers".

If you have a favorite discovery you would be willing to share with other travellers who love to travel the "inn way", please let us hear from you and include the following information:

1. *Your name, address and telephone number.*

2. *Name, address and telephone number of "your inn".*

3. *Brochure or picture of inn (we cannot return material).*

4. *Written permission to use an edited version of your description.*

5. *Would you want your name, city and state included in the book?*

We are constantly updating and revising all of our guide books. We would appreciate comments on any of your favorites. The types of inns we would love to hear about are those with special old-world ambiance, charm and atmosphere. We need a brochure or picture so that we can select those which most closely follow the mood of our guides. We look forward to hearing from you. Thank you.

Karen Brown's Country Inn Guides

The Most Reliable & Informative Series on Country Inns

Detailed itineraries guide you through the countryside **and suggest a cozy inn** for each night's stay. In the hotel section, every listing has been inspected **and chosen** for its romantic ambiance. Charming accommodations reflect every price range, from budget hideaways to deluxe palaces.

Order Form

KAREN BROWN'S COUNTRY INN GUIDES

Please ask in your local bookstore for KAREN BROWN'S COUNTRY INN guides.
If the books you want are unavailable, you may order directly from the publisher.

AUSTRIAN COUNTRY INNS & CASTLES $12.95

CALIFORNIA COUNTRY INNS & ITINERARIES $12.95

ENGLISH, WELSH & SCOTTISH COUNTRY INNS $12.95

EUROPEAN COUNTRY CUISINE - ROMANTIC INNS & RECIPES $10.95

EUROPEAN COUNTRY INNS - BEST ON A BUDGET $14.95

FRENCH COUNTRY BED & BREAKFASTS $12.95

FRENCH COUNTRY INNS & CHATEAUX $12.95

GERMAN COUNTRY INNS & CASTLES $12.95

IRISH COUNTRY INNS $12.95

ITALIAN COUNTRY INNS & VILLAS $12.95

PORTUGUESE COUNTRY INNS & POUSADAS $12.95

SCANDINAVIAN COUNTRY INNS & MANORS $12.95

SPANISH COUNTRY INNS & PARADORS $12.95

SWISS COUNTRY INNS & CHALETS $12.95

Name _____ *Street* _____

City _____ *State* _____ *Zip* _____

Add $2.00 for the first book and .50 for each additional book for postage & packing.
California residents add 6 1/2% sales tax.
Indicate the number of copies of each title. Send in form with your check to:

KAREN BROWN'S COUNTRY INN GUIDES
P.O Box 70
San Mateo, CA 94401
(415) 342-9117

This guide is especially written for the individual traveller who wants to plan his own vacation. However, should you prefer to join a group, Town and Country - Hillsdale Travel can recommend tours using country inns with romantic ambiance for many of the nights' accommodation. Or, should you want to organize your own group (art class, gourmet society, bridge club, church group, etc.) and travel with friends, custom tours can be arranged using small hotels with special charm and appeal. For further information please call:

Town & Country - Hillsdale Travel
16 East Third Avenue
San Mateo, California 94401

(415) 342-5591
Outside California 800-227-6733

JUNE BROWN, who was born in Sheffield, England, has an extensive background in travel dating back to her school-girl days when she "youth hosteled" throughout Europe. When June moved to California, she worked as a travel consultant before joining her friend Karen to assist in the research, writing and production of her Country Inn guides. June now lives in the San Francisco Bay area with her husband, Tony, their teenage son, Simon, and baby daughter, Clare.

BARBARA TAPP, the talented professional artist who is responsible for most of the interior sketches in *California Country Inns & Itineraries*, always saves time from her busy art and homemaking schedule to help her friend Karen with the illustrations for her Country Inn guides. Born and raised in Sydney, Australia, Barbara now lives in the San Francisco Bay area with her husband, Richard, their two young sons, Jonathan and Alexander, and their baby daughter, Georgia.

Karen Brown (Herbert) was born in Denver, but has spent most of her life in the San Francisco Bay area where she now lives with her husband, Rick, their little girl, Alexandra, and baby son, Richard. Taking a year off from college, Karen travelled to Europe and wrote French Country Inns & Chateaux, the first in what has grown to be an extremely successful series of 14 guide books on charming places to stay. For many years Karen has been planning to open her own country inn. Her dream will soon come to reality - Karen and her husband, Rick, have bought a beautiful piece of property on the coast south of San Francisco and are working with an architect to design the "perfect" little inn which will be furnished with the antiques she has been collecting for many years and will incorporate her wealth of information on just what makes an inn very special. Karen and Rick are looking forward to welcoming guests and friends to their inn.